with

Internet Explorer 7.0
Getting Started

Shelley Gaskin and Susan K. Fry

PEARSON

Prentice
Hall

Upper Saddle River, New Jersey

This book is dedicated to my students, who inspire me every day, and to my husband, Fred Gaskin.
—Shelley Gaskin

To my family: Phil, Alex, Allie, Courtney and Candace without whose help and support I would never be able to pursue my interests in reviewing and writing chapters and supplements for Microsoft Office applications.
—Susan K. Fry

Library of Congress Cataloging-in-Publication Data

Gaskin, Shelley.
  Go! Getting started with Internet 7.0 / Shelley Gaskin and Susan K. Fry.
    p. cm.
  Includes index.
  ISBN 0-13-157244-X
  1. Microsoft Internet explorer. 2. Browsers (Computer programs) I. Fry, Susan K. II. Title.
  TK5105.883.M53G39 2008
  005.7'1376--dc22

                                                                2007009637

Vice President and Publisher: Natalie E. Anderson
Associate VP/Executive Acquisitions Editor, Print: Stephanie Wall
Executive Acquisitions Editor, Media: Richard Keaveny
Product Development Manager: Eileen Bien Calabro Sr.
Editorial Project Manager: Laura Burgess
Development Editor: Ginny Munroe
Editorial Assistants: Becky Knauer, Lora Cimiluca
Content Development Manager: Cathi Profitko
Production Media Project Manager: Lorena Cerisano
Senior Media Project Manager: Steve Gagliostro
Director of Marketing: Margaret Waples
Senior Marketing Manager: Jason Sakos
Sales Associate: Rebecca Scott
Managing Editor: Lynda J. Castillo

Production Project Manager/Buyer: Wanda Rockwell
Production Editor: GGS Book Services
Photo Researcher: GGS Book Services
Manufacturing Buyer: Natacha Moore
Production/Editorial Assistant: Sandra K. Bernales
Design Director: Maria Lange
Art Director/Interior Design: Blair Brown
Cover Photo: Courtesy of Getty Images, Inc./Marvin Mattelson
Composition: GGS Book Services
Project Management: GGS Book Services
Cover Printer: Phoenix Color
Printer/Binder: RR Donnelley/Willard

Microsoft, Windows, Word, PowerPoint, Outlook, FrontPage, Visual Basic, MSN, The Microsoft Network, and/or other Microsoft products referenced herein are either trademarks or registered trademarks of Microsoft Corporation in the U.S.A. and other countries. Screen shots and icons reprinted with permission from the Microsoft Corporation. This book is not sponsored or endorsed by or affiliated with Microsoft Corporation.

Credits and acknowledgments borrowed from other sources and reproduced, with permission, in this textbook are as follows or on the appropriate page within the text.

    Page 2: Getty Images, Inc.

V0N4   10 9 8
ISBN-10: 0-13-157244-X
ISBN-13: 978-0-13-157244-7

Table of Contents

Letter from the Editor

Dear Instructors and Students,

The primary goal of the *GO!* Series is two-fold. The first goal is to help instructors teach the course they want in less time. The second goal is to provide students with the skills to solve business problems using the computer as a tool, for both themselves and the organization for which they might be employed.

The *GO!* Series was originally created by Series Editor Shelley Gaskin and published with the release of Microsoft Office 2003. Her ideas came from years of using textbooks that didn't meet all the needs of today's diverse classroom and that were too confusing for students. Shelley continues to enhance the series by ensuring we stay true to our vision of developing quality instruction and useful classroom tools.

But we also need your input and ideas.

Over time, the *GO!* Series has evolved based on direct feedback from instructors and students using the series. *We are the publisher that listens*. To publish a textbook that works for you, it's critical that we continue to listen to this feedback. It's important to me to talk with you and hear your stories about using *GO!* Your voice can make a difference.

My hope is that this letter will inspire you to write me an e-mail and share your thoughts on using the *GO!* Series.

Stephanie Wall
Executive Editor, *GO!* Series
stephanie_wall@prenhall.com

GO! System Contributors

We thank the following people for their hard work and support in making the *GO!* System all that it is!

Additional Author Support

Coyle, Diane	Montgomery County Community College
Fry, Susan	Boise State
Townsend, Kris	Spokane Falls Community College
Stroup, Tracey	Amgen Corporation

Instructor Resource Authors

Amer, Beverly	Northern Arizona University	Paterson, Jim	Paradise Valley Community College
Boito, Nancy	Harrisburg Area Community College	Prince, Lisa	Missouri State
Coyle, Diane	Montgomery County Community College	Rodgers, Gwen	Southern Nazarene University
Dawson, Tamara	Southern Nazarene University	Ruymann, Amy	Burlington Community College
Driskel, Loretta	Niagara County Community College	Ryan, Bob	Montgomery County Community College
Elliott, Melissa	Odessa College		
Fry, Susan	Boise State	Smith, Diane	Henry Ford College
Geoghan, Debra	Bucks County Community College	Spangler, Candice	Columbus State Community College
Hearn, Barbara	Community College of Philadelphia	Thompson, Joyce	Lehigh Carbon Community College
Jones, Stephanie	South Plains College	Tiffany, Janine	Reading Area Community College
Madsen, Donna	Kirkwood Community College	Watt, Adrienne	Douglas College
Meck, Kari	Harrisburg Area Community College	Weaver, Paul	Bossier Parish Community College
Miller, Cindy	Ivy Tech	Weber, Sandy	Gateway Technical College
Nowakowski, Tony	Buffalo State	Wood, Dawn	
Pace, Phyllis	Queensborough Community College	Weissman, Jonathan	Finger Lakes Community College

Super Reviewers

Brotherton, Cathy	Riverside Community College	Maurer, Trina	Odessa College
Cates, Wally	Central New Mexico Community College	Meck, Kari	Harrisburg Area Community College
		Miller, Cindy	Ivy Tech Community College
Cone, Bill	Northern Arizona University	Nielson, Phil	Salt Lake Community College
Coverdale, John	Riverside Community College	Rodgers, Gwen	Southern Nazarene University
Foster, Nancy	Baker College	Smolenski, Robert	Delaware Community College
Helfand, Terri	Chaffey College	Spangler, Candice	Columbus State Community College
Hibbert, Marilyn	Salt Lake Community College	Thompson, Joyce	Lehigh Carbon Community College
Holliday, Mardi	Community College of Philadelphia	Weber, Sandy	Gateway Technical College
Jerry, Gina	Santa Monica College	Wells, Lorna	Salt Lake Community College
Martin, Carol	Harrisburg Area Community College	Zaboski, Maureen	University of Scranton

Technical Editors

Janice Snyder
Joyce Nielsen
Colette Eisele
Janet Pickard
Mara Zebest
Lindsey Allen
William Daley

Student Reviewers

Allen, John	Asheville-Buncombe Tech Community College	Erickson, Mike	Ball State University
		Gadomski, Amanda	Northern Michigan University
Alexander, Steven	St. Johns River Community College	Gyselinck, Craig	Central Washington University
Alexander, Melissa	Tulsa Community College	Harrison, Margo	Central Washington University
Bolz, Stephanie	Northern Michigan University	Heacox, Kate	Central Washington University
Berner, Ashley	Central Washington University	Hill, Cheretta	Northwestern State University
Boomer, Michelle	Northern Michigan University	Innis, Tim	Tulsa Community College
Busse, Brennan	Northern Michigan University	Jarboe, Aaron	Central Washington University
Butkey, Maura	Central Washington University	Klein, Colleen	Northern Michigan University
Christensen, Kaylie	Northern Michigan University	Moeller, Jeffrey	Northern Michigan University
Connally, Brianna	Central Washington University	Nicholson, Regina	Athens Tech College
Davis, Brandon	Northern Michigan University	Niehaus, Kristina	Northern Michigan University
Davis, Christen	Central Washington University	Nisa, Zaibun	Santa Rosa Community College
Den Boer, Lance	Central Washington University	Nunez, Nohelia	Santa Rosa Community College
Dix, Jessica	Central Washington University	Oak, Samantha	Central Washington University
Moeller, Jeffrey	Northern Michigan University	Oertii, Monica	Central Washington University
Downs, Elizabeth	Central Washington University	Palenshus, Juliet	Central Washington University

Pohl, Amanda	Northern Michigan University	Shanahan, Megan	Northern Michigan University
Presnell, Randy	Central Washington University	Teska, Erika	Hawaii Pacific University
Ritner, April	Northern Michigan University	Traub, Amy	Northern Michigan University
Rodriguez, Flavia	Northwestern State University	Underwood, Katie	Central Washington University
Roberts, Corey	Tulsa Community College	Walters, Kim	Central Washington University
Rossi, Jessica Ann	Central Washington University	Wilson, Kelsie	Central Washington University
Shafapay, Natasha	Central Washington University	Wilson, Amanda	Green River Community College

Series Reviewers

Abraham, Reni	Houston Community College	Crawford, Thomasina	Miami-Dade College, Kendall Campus
Agatston, Ann	Agatston Consulting Technical College	Credico, Grace	Lethbridge Community College
		Crenshaw, Richard	Miami Dade Community College, North
Alexander, Melody	Ball Sate University		
Alejandro, Manuel	Southwest Texas Junior College	Crespo, Beverly	Mt. San Antonio College
Ali, Farha	Lander University	Crossley, Connie	Cincinnati State Technical Community College
Amici, Penny	Harrisburg Area Community College		
Anderson, Patty A.	Lake City Community College	Curik, Mary	Central New Mexico Community College
Andrews, Wilma	Virginia Commonwealth College, Nebraska University		
		De Arazoza, Ralph	Miami Dade Community College
Anik, Mazhar	Tiffin University	Danno, John	DeVry University/Keller Graduate School
Armstrong, Gary	Shippensburg University		
Atkins, Bonnie	Delaware Technical Community College	Davis, Phillip	Del Mar College
		DeHerrera, Laurie	Pikes Peak Community College
Bachand, LaDonna	Santa Rosa Community College	Delk, Dr. K. Kay	Seminole Community College
Bagui, Sikha	University of West Florida	Doroshow, Mike	Eastfield College
Beecroft, Anita	Kwantlen University College	Douglas, Gretchen	SUNYCortland
Bell, Paula	Lock Haven College	Dove, Carol	Community College of Allegheny
Belton, Linda	Springfield Tech. Community College	Driskel, Loretta	Niagara Community College
		Duckwiler, Carol	Wabaunsee Community College
Bennett, Judith	Sam Houston State University	Duncan, Mimi	University of Missouri-St. Louis
Bhatia, Sai	Riverside Community College	Duthie, Judy	Green River Community College
Bishop, Frances	DeVry Institute—Alpharetta (ATL)	Duvall, Annette	Central New Mexico Community College
Blaszkiewicz, Holly	Ivy Tech Community College/Region 1		
Branigan, Dave	DeVry University	Ecklund, Paula	Duke University
Bray, Patricia	Allegany College of Maryland	Eng, Bernice	Brookdale Community College
Brotherton, Cathy	Riverside Community College	Evans, Billie	Vance-Granville Community College
Buehler, Lesley	Ohlone College	Feuerbach, Lisa	Ivy Tech East Chicago
Buell, C	Central Oregon Community College	Fisher, Fred	Florida State University
Byars, Pat	Brookhaven College	Foster, Penny L.	Anne Arundel Community College
Byrd, Lynn	Delta State University, Cleveland, Mississippi	Foszcz, Russ	McHenry County College
		Fry, Susan	Boise State University
Cacace, Richard N.	Pensacola Junior College	Fustos, Janos	Metro State
Cadenhead, Charles	Brookhaven College	Gallup, Jeanette	Blinn College
Calhoun, Ric	Gordon College	Gelb, Janet	Grossmont College
Cameron, Eric	Passaic Community College	Gentry, Barb	Parkland College
Carriker, Sandra	North Shore Community College	Gerace, Karin	St. Angela Merici School
Cannamore, Madie	Kennedy King	Gerace, Tom	Tulane University
Carreon, Cleda	Indiana University—Purdue University, Indianapolis	Ghajar, Homa	Oklahoma State University
		Gifford, Steve	Northwest Iowa Community College
Chaffin, Catherine	Shawnee State University	Glazer, Ellen	Broward Community College
Chauvin, Marg	Palm Beach Community College, Boca Raton	Gordon, Robert	Hofstra University
		Gramlich, Steven	Pasco-Hernando Community College
Challa, Chandrashekar	Virginia State University	Graviett, Nancy M.	St. Charles Community College, St. Peters, Missouri
Chamlou, Afsaneh	NOVA Alexandria		
Chapman, Pam	Wabaunsee Community College	Greene, Rich	Community College of Allegheny County
Christensen, Dan	Iowa Western Community College		
Clay, Betty	Southeastern Oklahoma State University	Gregoryk, Kerry	Virginia Commonwealth State
		Griggs, Debra	Bellevue Community College
Collins, Linda D.	Mesa Community College	Grimm, Carol	Palm Beach Community College
Conroy-Link, Janet	Holy Family College	Hahn, Norm	Thomas Nelson Community College
Cosgrove, Janet	Northwestern CT Community	Hammerschlag, Dr. Bill	Brookhaven College
Courtney, Kevin	Hillsborough Community College	Hansen, Michelle	Davenport University
Cox, Rollie	Madison Area Technical College	Hayden, Nancy	Indiana University—Purdue University, Indianapolis
Crawford, Hiram	Olive Harvey College		

Hayes, Theresa	Broward Community College	Lord, Alexandria	Asheville Buncombe Tech
Helfand, Terri	Chaffey College	Lowe, Rita	Harold Washington College
Helms, Liz	Columbus State Community College	Low, Willy Hui	Joliet Junior College
Hernandez, Leticia	TCI College of Technology	Lucas, Vickie	Broward Community College
Hibbert, Marilyn	Salt Lake Community College	Lynam, Linda	Central Missouri State University
Hoffman, Joan	Milwaukee Area Technical College	Lyon, Lynne	Durham College
Hogan, Pat	Cape Fear Community College	Lyon, Pat Rajski	Tomball College
Holland, Susan	Southeast Community College	MacKinnon, Ruth	Georgia Southern University
Hopson, Bonnie	Athens Technical College	Macon, Lisa	Valencia Community College, West Campus
Horvath, Carrie	Albertus Magnus College		
Horwitz, Steve	Community College of Philadelphia	Machuca, Wayne	College of the Sequoias
Hotta, Barbara	Leeward Community College	Madison, Dana	Clarion University
Howard, Bunny	St. Johns River Community	Maguire, Trish	Eastern New Mexico University
Howard, Chris	DeVry University	Malkan, Rajiv	Montgomery College
Huckabay, Jamie	Austin Community College	Manning, David	Northern Kentucky University
Hudgins, Susan	East Central University	Marcus, Jacquie	Niagara Community College
Hulett, Michelle J.	Missouri State University	Marghitu, Daniela	Auburn University
Hunt, Darla A.	Morehead State University, Morehead, Kentucky	Marks, Suzanne	Bellevue Community College
		Marquez, Juanita	El Centro College
Hunt, Laura	Tulsa Community College	Marquez, Juan	Mesa Community College
Jacob, Sherry	Jefferson Community College	Martyn, Margie	Baldwin-Wallace College
Jacobs, Duane	Salt Lake Community College	Marucco, Toni	Lincoln Land Community College
Jauken, Barb	Southeastern Community	Mason, Lynn	Lubbock Christian University
Johnson, Kathy	Wright College	Matutis, Audrone	Houston Community College
Johnson, Mary	Kingwood College	Matkin, Marie	University of Lethbridge
Johnson, Mary	Mt. San Antonio College	McCain, Evelynn	Boise State University
Jones, Stacey	Benedict College	McCannon, Melinda	Gordon College
Jones, Warren	University of Alabama, Birmingham	McCarthy, Marguerite	Northwestern Business College
Jordan, Cheryl	San Juan College	McCaskill, Matt L.	Brevard Community College
Kapoor, Bhushan	California State University, Fullerton	McClellan, Carolyn	Tidewater Community College
Kasai, Susumu	Salt Lake Community College	McClure, Darlean	College of Sequoias
Kates, Hazel	Miami Dade Community College, Kendall	McCrory, Sue A.	Missouri State University
		McCue, Stacy	Harrisburg Area Community College
Keen, Debby	University of Kentucky	McEntire-Orbach, Teresa	Middlesex County College
Keeter, Sandy	Seminole Community College	McLeod, Todd	Fresno City College
Kern-Blystone, Dorothy Jean	Bowling Green State	McManus, Illyana	Grossmont College
		McPherson, Dori	Schoolcraft College
Keskin, Ilknur	The University of South Dakota	Meiklejohn, Nancy	Pikes Peak Community College
Kirk, Colleen	Mercy College	Menking, Rick	Hardin-Simmons University
Kleckner, Michelle	Elon University	Meredith, Mary	University of Louisiana at Lafayette
Kliston, Linda	Broward Community College, North Campus	Mermelstein, Lisa	Baruch College
		Metos, Linda	Salt Lake Community College
Kochis, Dennis	Suffolk County Community College	Meurer, Daniel	University of Cincinnati
Kramer, Ed	Northern Virginia Community College	Meyer, Marian	Central New Mexico Community College
Laird, Jeff	Northeast State Community College	Miller, Cindy	Ivy Tech Community College, Lafayette, Indiana
Lamoureaux, Jackie	Central New Mexico Community College		
		Mitchell, Susan	Davenport University
Lange, David	Grand Valley State	Mohle, Dennis	Fresno Community College
LaPointe, Deb	Central New Mexico Community College	Monk, Ellen	University of Delaware
		Moore, Rodney	Holland College
Larson, Donna	Louisville Technical Institute	Morris, Mike	Southeastern Oklahoma State University
Laspina, Kathy	Vance-Granville Community College		
Le Grand, Dr. Kate	Broward Community College	Morris, Nancy	Hudson Valley Community College
Lenhart, Sheryl	Terra Community College	Moseler, Dan	Harrisburg Area Community College
Letavec, Chris	University of Cincinnati	Nabors, Brent	Reedley College, Clovis Center
Liefert, Jane	Everett Community College	Nadas, Erika	Wright College
Lindaman, Linda	Black Hawk Community College	Nadelman, Cindi	New England College
Lindberg, Martha	Minnesota State University	Nademlynsky, Lisa	Johnson & Wales University
Lightner, Renee	Broward Community College	Ncube, Cathy	University of West Florida
Lindberg, Martha	Minnesota State University	Nagengast, Joseph	Florida Career College
Linge, Richard	Arizona Western College	Newsome, Eloise	Northern Virginia Community College Woodbridge
Logan, Mary G.	Delgado Community College		
Loizeaux, Barbara	Westchester Community College	Nicholls, Doreen	Mohawk Valley Community College
Lopez, Don	Clovis-State Center Community College District	Nunan, Karen	Northeast State Technical Community College

Odegard, Teri	Edmonds Community College	Sterling, Janet	Houston Community College
Ogle, Gregory	North Community College	Stoughton, Catherine	Laramie County Community College
Orr, Dr. Claudia	Northern Michigan University South	Sullivan, Angela	Joliet Junior College
Otieno, Derek	DeVry University	Szurek, Joseph	University of Pittsburgh at Greensburg
Otton, Diana Hill	Chesapeake College		
Oxendale, Lucia	West Virginia Institute of Technology	Tarver, Mary Beth	Northwestern State University
		Taylor, Michael	Seattle Central Community College
Paiano, Frank	Southwestern College	Thangiah, Sam	Slippery Rock University
Patrick, Tanya	Clackamas Community College	Thompson-Sellers, Ingrid	Georgia Perimeter College
Peairs, Deb	Clark State Community College	Tomasi, Erik	Baruch College
Prince, Lisa	Missouri State University-Springfield Campus	Toreson, Karen	Shoreline Community College
		Trifiletti, John J.	Florida Community College at Jacksonville
Proietti, Kathleen	Northern Essex Community College		
Pusins, Delores	HCCC	Trivedi, Charulata	Quinsigamond Community College, Woodbridge
Raghuraman, Ram	Joliet Junior College		
Reasoner, Ted Allen	Indiana University—Purdue	Tucker, William	Austin Community College
Reeves, Karen	High Point University	Turgeon, Cheryl	Asnuntuck Community College
Remillard, Debbie	New Hampshire Technical Institute	Turpen, Linda	Central New Mexico Community College
Rhue, Shelly	DeVry University		
Richards, Karen	Maplewoods Community College	Upshaw, Susan	Del Mar College
Richardson, Mary	Albany Technical College	Unruh, Angela	Central Washington University
Rodgers, Gwen	Southern Nazarene University	Vanderhoof, Dr. Glenna	Missouri State University-Springfield Campus
Roselli, Diane	Harrisburg Area Community College		
Ross, Dianne	University of Louisiana in Lafayette	Vargas, Tony	El Paso Community College
Rousseau, Mary	Broward Community College, South	Vicars, Mitzi	Hampton University
Samson, Dolly	Hawaii Pacific University	Villarreal, Kathleen	Fresno
Sams, Todd	University of Cincinnati	Vitrano, Mary Ellen	Palm Beach Community College
Sandoval, Everett	Reedley College	Volker, Bonita	Tidewater Community College
Sardone, Nancy	Seton Hall University	Wahila, Lori (Mindy)	Tompkins Cortland Community College
Scafide, Jean	Mississippi Gulf Coast Community College		
		Waswick, Kim	Southeast Community College, Nebraska
Scheeren, Judy	Westmoreland County Community College		
		Wavle, Sharon	Tompkins Cortland Community College
Schneider, Sol	Sam Houston State University		
Scroggins, Michael	Southwest Missouri State University	Webb, Nancy	City College of San Francisco
Sever, Suzanne	Northwest Arkansas Community College	Wells, Barbara E.	Central Carolina Technical College
		Wells, Lorna	Salt Lake Community College
Sheridan, Rick	California State University-Chico	Welsh, Jean	Lansing Community College Nebraska
Silvers, Pamela	Asheville Buncombe Tech		
Singer, Steven A.	University of Hawai'i, Kapi'olani Community College	White, Bruce	Quinnipiac University
		Willer, Ann	Solano Community College
Sinha, Atin	Albany State University	Williams, Mark	Lane Community College
Skolnick, Martin	Florida Atlantic University	Wilson, Kit	Red River College
Smith, T. Michael	Austin Community College	Wilson, Roger	Fairmont State University
Smith, Tammy	Tompkins Cortland Community Collge	Wimberly, Leanne	International Academy of Design and Technology
Smolenski, Bob	Delaware County Community College	Worthington, Paula	Northern Virginia Community College
Spangler, Candice	Columbus State		
Stedham, Vicki	St. Petersburg College, Clearwater	Yauney, Annette	Herkimer County Community College
Stefanelli, Greg	Carroll Community College		
Steiner, Ester	New Mexico State University	Yip, Thomas	Passaic Community College
Stenlund, Neal	Northern Virginia Community College, Alexandria	Zavala, Ben	Webster Tech
		Zlotow, Mary Ann	College of DuPage
St. John, Steve	Tulsa Community College	Zudeck, Steve	Broward Community College, North

About the Authors

Shelley Gaskin, Series Editor, is a professor of business and computer technology at Pasadena City College in Pasadena, California. She holds a master's degree in business education from Northern Illinois University and a doctorate in adult and community education from Ball State University. Dr. Gaskin has 15 years of experience in the computer industry with several Fortune 500 companies and has developed and written training materials for custom systems applications in both the public and private sector. She is also the author of books on Microsoft Outlook and word processing.

Susan K. Fry is a special lecturer in the College of Business and Economics at Boise State University, where she has taught full time since 1995. Susan received her bachelor's degree in business education from Fort Hays State University in Kansas in 1975 and a master's degree in finance from Louisiana State University in 1983. Susan teaches the Introductory Computer Application classes as well as the first-and second-semester business statistics courses. She enjoys reviewing manuscripts and writing chapters, supplements, and problems for new Office applications.

Susan spends most of her free time with her husband, Phil, and her four children, Alex, 15; Allie, 14; and twins Courtney and Candace, 7.

Visual Walk-Through of the *GO!* System

The *GO!* System is designed for ease of implementation on the instructor side and ease of understanding on the student. It has been completely developed based on professor and student feedback.

The *GO!* System is divided into three categories that reflect how you might organize your course—Prepare, Teach, and Assess.

Prepare

GO!

Because the GO! System was designed and written by instructors like yourself, it includes the tools that allow you to Prepare, Teach, and Assess in your course. We have organized the GO! System into these three categories that match how you work through your course and thus, it's even easier for you to implement.

To help you get started, here is an outline of the first activities you may want to do in order to conduct your course.

There are several other tools not listed here that are available in the GO! System so please refer to your GO! Guide for a complete listing of all the tools.

Prepare
1. Prepare the course syllabus
2. Plan the course assignments
3. Organize the student resources

Teach
4. Conduct demonstrations and lectures

Assess
5. Assign and grade assignments, quizzes, tests, and assessments

PREPARE

1. Prepare the course syllabus
A syllabus template is provided on the IRCD in the **go07_syllabus_template** folder of the main directory. It includes a course calendar planner for 8-week, 12-week, and 16-week formats. Depending on your term (summer or regular semester) you can modify one of these according to your course plan, and then add information pertinent to your course and institution.

2. Plan course assignments
For each chapter, an Assignment Sheet listing every in-chapter and end-of-chapter project is located on the IRCD within the **go01_gofoffice2007intro_instructor_resources_by_chapter** folder. From there, navigate to the specific chapter folder. These sheets are Word tables, so you can delete rows for the projects that you choose not to assign or add rows for your own assignments—if any. There is a column to add the number of points you want to assign to each project depending on your grading scheme. At the top of the sheet, you can fill in the course information.

Transitioning to GO! Office 2007   Page 1 of 1

NEW

Transition Guide
New to *GO!*—We've made it quick and easy to plan the format and activities for your class.

GO! with Microsoft Office 2007 Introductory
SAMPLE SYLLABUS (16 weeks)

I. COURSE INFORMATION

Course No.:	Semester:
Course Title:	Credits:
Course Hours:	

Instructor:	Office:
Office Hours:	
Email:	Phone:

II. TEXT AND MATERIALS
Before starting the course, you will need the following:

> GO! with Microsoft Office 2007 Introductory by Shelley Gaskin, Robert L. Ferrett, Alicia Vargas, Suzanne Marks ©2007, published by Pearson Prentice Hall.
> ISBN 0-13-167990-6

> Storage device for saving files (any of the following: multiple diskettes, CD-RW, flash drive, etc.)

III. WHAT YOU WILL LEARN IN THIS COURSE
This is a hands-on course where you will learn to use a computer to practice the most commonly used Microsoft programs including the Windows operating system, Internet Explorer for navigating the Internet, Outlook for managing your personal information and the four most popular programs within the Microsoft Office Suite (Word, Excel, PowerPoint and Access). You will also practice the basics of using a computer, mouse and keyboard. You will learn to be an intermediate level user of the Microsoft Office Suite.

Within the Microsoft Office Suite, you will use Word, Excel, PowerPoint, and Access. Microsoft Word is a word processing program with which you can create common business and personal documents. Microsoft Excel is a spreadsheet program that organizes and calculates accounting-type information. Microsoft PowerPoint is a presentation graphics program with which you can develop slides to accompany an oral presentation. Finally, Microsoft Access is a database program that organizes large amounts of information in a useful manner.

Syllabus Template
Includes course calendar planner for 8-,12-, and 16-week formats.

Assignment Sheet

One per chapter. Lists all possible assignments; add to and delete from this simple Word table according to your course plan.

GO! with Microsoft Office 2007 Introductory

Assignment Sheet for GO! with Microsoft Office 2007 Introductory
Chapter 5

Instructor Name: _____
Course Information: _____

Do This (✓ when done)	Then Hand in This Check each Project for the elements listed on the Assignment Tag. Attach the Tag to your Project.	Submit Printed Formulas	By This Date	Possible Points	Your Points
Study the text and perform the steps for Activities 5.1 – 5.11	Project 5A Application Letter				
Study the text and perform the steps for Activities 5.12 – 5.20	Project 5B Company Overview				
End-of-Chapter Assessments					
Complete the Matching and Fill-In-the-Blank questions	As directed by your instructor				
Complete Project 5C	Project 5C Receipt Letter				
Complete Project 5D	Project 5D Marketing				
Complete Project 5E	Project 5E School Tour				
Complete Project 5F	Project 5F Scouting Trip				
Complete Project 5G	Project 5G Contract				
Complete Project 5H	Project 5H Invitation				
Complete Project 5I	Project 5I Fax Cover				
Complete Project 5J	Project 5J Business Running Case				
Complete Project 5K	Project 5K Services				
Complete Project 5L	Project 5L Survey Form				
Complete Project 5M	Project 5M Press Release				

Copyright © 2008 Pearson Prentice Hall — Page 1 of 1

File Guide to the GO! Supplements

Tabular listing of all supplements and their file names.

GO! with Microsoft Office 2007
Supplements File Guide - Assess & Grade

Assignment Planning Guide

Description of GO! assignments with recommendations based on class size, delivery mode, and student needs. Includes examples from fellow instructors.

NEW

GO! with Microsoft Office 2007 Introductory
Assignment Planning Guide

Planning the Course Assignments

For each chapter in GO!, an Assignment Sheet listing every in-chapter and end-of-chapter project is located on the IRCD. These sheets are Word tables, so you can delete rows for the projects that you will not assign, and then add rows for any of your own assignments that you may have developed. There is a column to add the number of points you want to assign to each project—depending on your grading scheme. At the top of the sheet, you can fill in your course information.

Additionally, for each chapter, student Assignment Tags are provided for every project (including Problem Solving projects)—also located on the IRCD. These are small scoring checklists on which you can check off errors made by the student, and with which the student can verify that all project elements are complete. For campus classes, the student can attach the tags to his or her paper submissions. For online classes, many GO! instructors have the student include these with the electronic submission.

Deciding What to Assign

Front Portion of the Chapter—Instructional Projects: The projects in the front portion of the chapter, which are listed on the first page of each chapter, are the instructional projects. Most instructors assign all of these projects, because this is where the student receives the instruction and engages in the active learning.

End-of-Chapter—Practice and Critical Thinking Projects: In the back portion of the chapter (the gray pages), you can assign on a prescriptive basis; that is, for students who were challenged by the instructional projects, you might assign one or more projects from the two *Skills Reviews*, which provide maximum prompting and a thorough review of the entire chapter. For students who have previous software knowledge and who completed the instructional projects easily, you might assign only the *Mastery Projects*.

You can also assign prescriptively by Objective, because each end-of-chapter project indicates the Objectives covered. So you might assign, on a student-by-student basis, only the projects that cover the Objectives with which the student seemed to have difficulty in the instructional projects.

The five Problem Solving projects and the You and GO! project are the authentic assessments that pull together the student's learning. Here the student is presented with a "messy real-life situation" and then uses his or her knowledge and skill to solve a problem, produce a product, give a presentation, or demonstrate a procedure. You might assign one or more of the Problem

GO! Assignment Planning Guide — Page 1 of 1

Student Data Files

Online Study Guide for Students

Interactive objective-style questions based on chapter content.

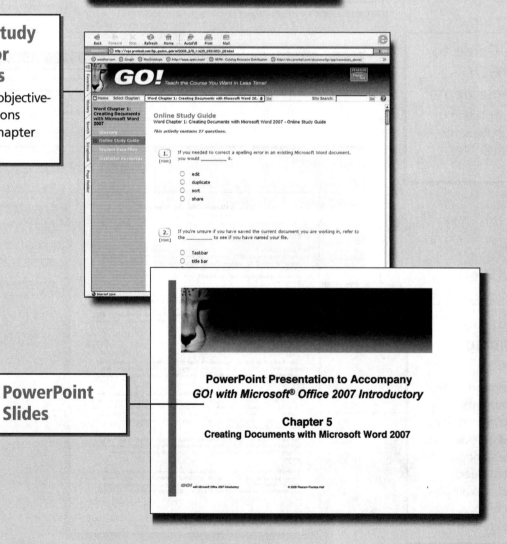

PowerPoint Slides

Teach

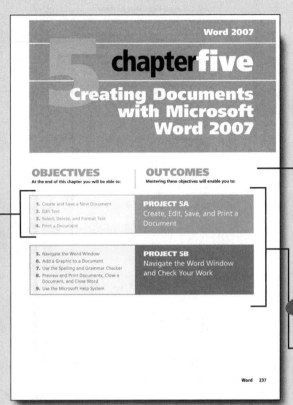

Learning Objectives and Student Outcomes

Objectives are clustered around projects that result in student outcomes. They help students learn how to solve problems, not just learn software features.

Project-Based Instruction

Students do not practice features of the application; they create real projects that they will need in the real world. Projects are color coded for easy reference and are named to reflect skills the students will be practicing.

A and B Projects

Each chapter contains two instructional projects—A and B.

Each chapter opens with a story that sets the stage for the projects the student will create; the instruction does not force the student to pretend to be someone or make up a scenario.

Each chapter has an introductory paragraph that briefs students on what is important.

Visual Summary

Shows students upfront what their projects will look like when they are done.

Project Summary

Stated clearly and quickly in one paragraph.

NEW

File Guide

Clearly shows students which files are needed for the project and the names they will use to save their documents.

Objective

The skills the student will learn are clearly stated at the beginning of each project and color coded to match projects listed on the chapter opener page.

KEY FEATURE

GO!

Teachable Moment

Expository text is woven into the steps—at the moment students need to know it—not chunked together in a block of text that will go unread.

NEW

Screen Shots

Larger screen shots.

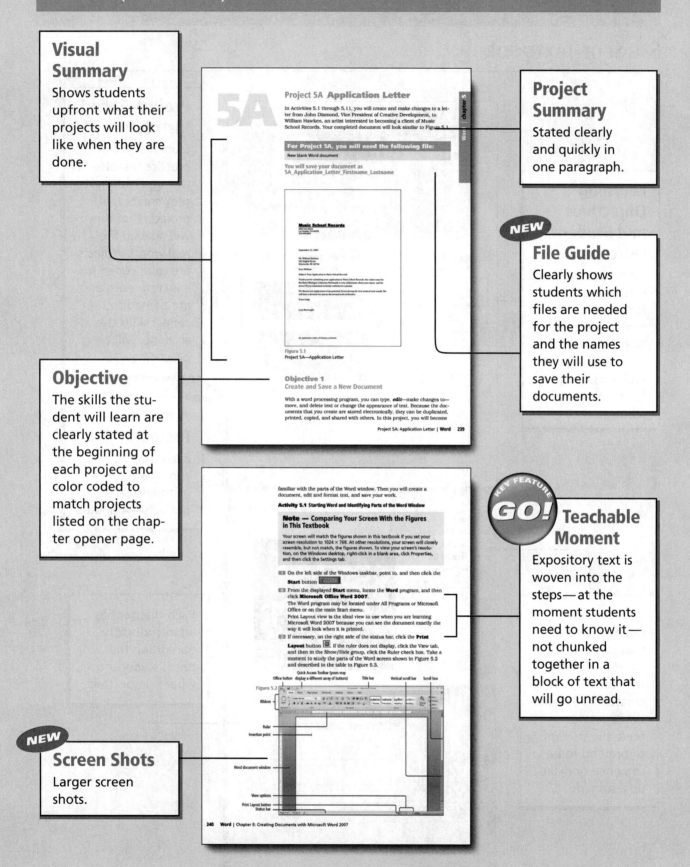

Steps

Color coded to the current project, easy to read, and not too many to confuse the student or too few to be meaningless.

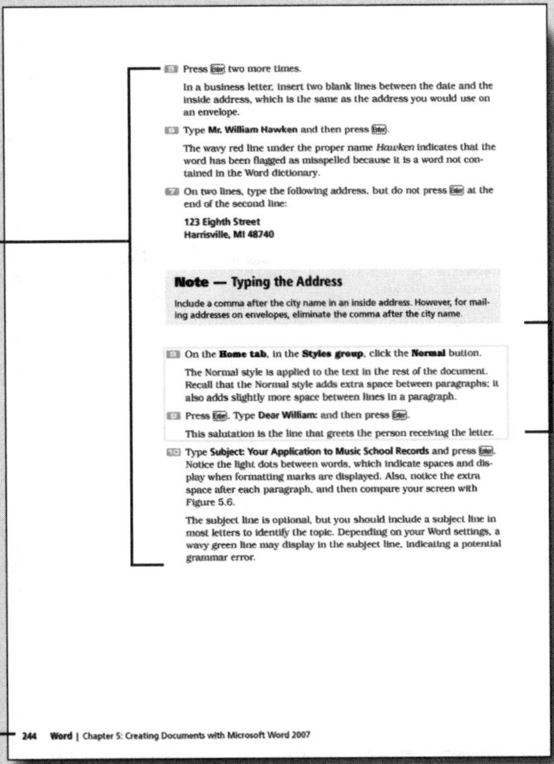

GO! KEY FEATURE
Sequential Pagination

No more confusing letters and abbreviations.

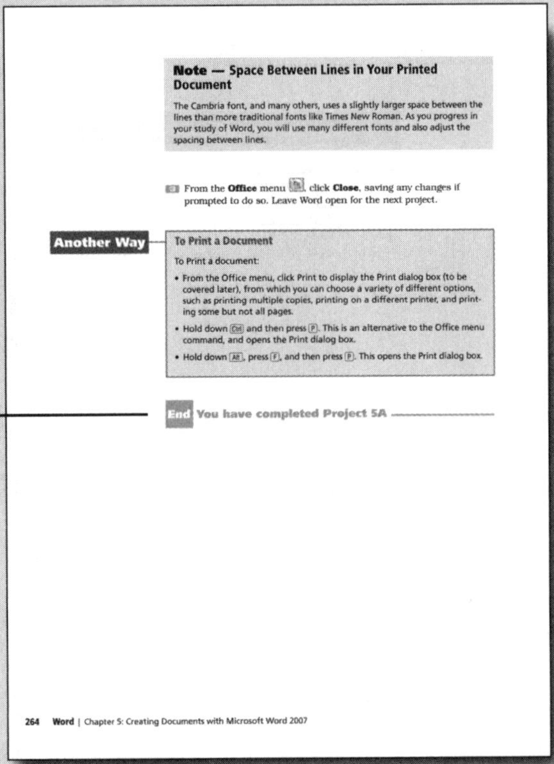

[Textbook page 244 excerpt]

Press Enter two more times.

In a business letter, insert two blank lines between the date and the inside address, which is the same as the address you would use on an envelope.

Type **Mr. William Hawken** and then press Enter.

The wavy red line under the proper name *Hawken* indicates that the word has been flagged as misspelled because it is a word not contained in the Word dictionary.

On two lines, type the following address, but do not press Enter at the end of the second line:

123 Eighth Street
Harrisville, MI 48740

Note — Typing the Address

Include a comma after the city name in an inside address. However, for mailing addresses on envelopes, eliminate the comma after the city name.

On the **Home tab**, in the **Styles group**, click the **Normal** button.

The Normal style is applied to the text in the rest of the document. Recall that the Normal style adds extra space between paragraphs; it also adds slightly more space between lines in a paragraph.

Press Enter. Type **Dear William:** and then press Enter.

This salutation is the line that greets the person receiving the letter.

Type **Subject: Your Application to Music School Records** and press Enter. Notice the light dots between words, which indicate spaces and display when formatting marks are displayed. Also, notice the extra space after each paragraph, and then compare your screen with Figure 5.6.

The subject line is optional, but you should include a subject line in most letters to identify the topic. Depending on your Word settings, a wavy green line may display in the subject line, indicating a potential grammar error.

GO! KEY FEATURE
Microsoft Procedural Syntax

All steps are written in Microsoft Procedural Syntax to put the student in the right place at the right time.

[Textbook page 264 excerpt]

Note — Space Between Lines in Your Printed Document

The Cambria font, and many others, uses a slightly larger space between the lines than more traditional fonts like Times New Roman. As you progress in your study of Word, you will use many different fonts and also adjust the spacing between lines.

From the **Office** menu, click **Close**, saving any changes if prompted to do so. Leave Word open for the next project.

Another Way

To Print a Document

To Print a document:

- From the Office menu, click Print to display the Print dialog box (to be covered later), from which you can choose a variety of different options, such as printing multiple copies, printing on a different printer, and printing some but not all pages.
- Hold down Ctrl and then press P. This is an alternative to the Office menu command, and opens the Print dialog box.
- Hold down Alt, press F, and then press P. This opens the Print dialog box.

End You have completed Project 5A

End-of-Project Icon

All projects in the *GO! Series* have clearly identifiable end points, useful in self-paced or online environments.

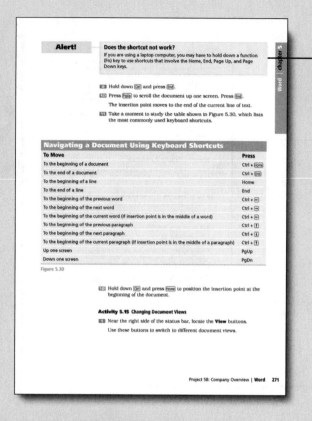

Alert box
Draws students' attention to make sure they aren't getting too far off course.

Another Way box
Shows students other ways of doing tasks.

More Knowledge box
Expands on a topic by going deeper into the material.

Note box
Points out important items to remember.

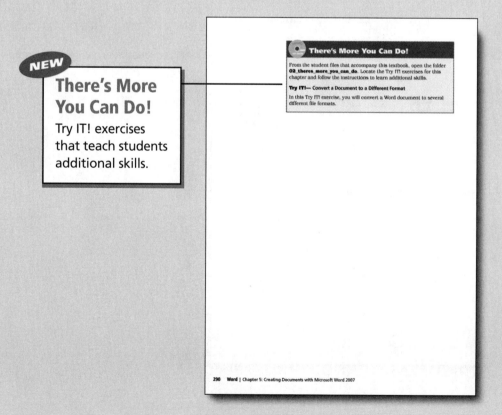

NEW

There's More You Can Do!
Try IT! exercises that teach students additional skills.

End-of-Chapter Material

Take your pick! Content-based or Outcomes-based projects to choose from. Below is a table outlining the various types of projects that fit into these two categories.

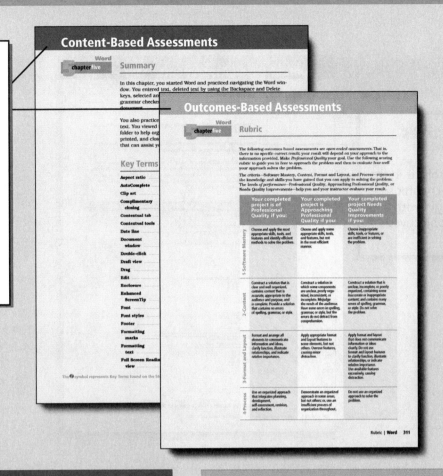

Content-Based Assessments
(Defined solutions with solution files provided for grading)

Project Letter	Name	Objectives Covered
N/A	Summary and Key Terms	
N/A	Multiple Choice	
N/A	Fill-in-the-blank	
C	Skills Review	Covers A Objectives
D	Skills Review	Covers B Objectives
E	Mastering Excel	Covers A Objectives
F	Mastering Excel	Covers B Objectives
G	Mastering Excel	Covers any combination of A and B Objectives
H	Mastering Excel	Covers any combination of A and B Objectives
I	Mastering Excel	Covers all A and B Objectives
J	Business Running Case	Covers all A and B Objectives

Outcomes-Based Assessments
(Open solutions that require a rubric for grading)

Project Letter	Name	Objectives Covered
N/A	Rubric	
K	Problem Solving	Covers as many Objectives from A and B as possible
L	Problem Solving	Covers as many Objectives from A and B as possible.
M	Problem Solving	Covers as many Objectives from A and B as possible.
N	Problem Solving	Covers as many Objectives from A and B as possible.
O	Problem Solving	Covers as many Objectives from A and B as possible.
P	You and GO!	Covers as many Objectives from A and B as possible
Q	GO! Help	Not tied to specific objectives
R	* Group Business Running Case	Covers A and B Objectives

* This project is provided only with the *GO! with Microsoft Office 2007 Introductory* book.

Objectives List

Most projects in the end-of-chapter section begin with a list of the objectives covered.

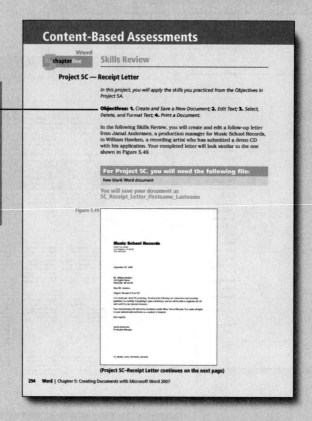

End of Each Project Clearly Marked

Clearly identified end points help separate the end-of-chapter projects.

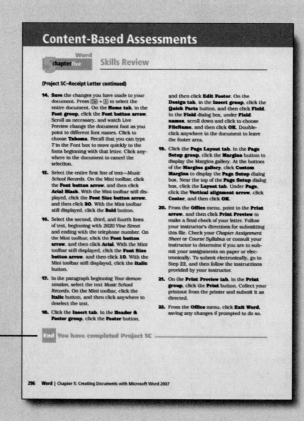

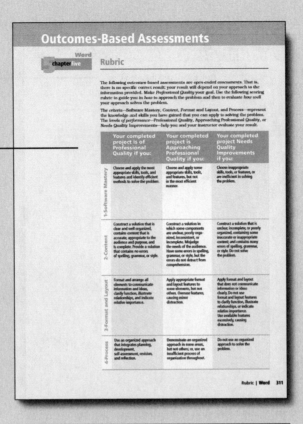

NEW

Rubric

A matrix that states the criteria and standards for grading student work. Used to grade open-ended assessments.

GO! with Help

Students practice using the Help feature of the Office application.

NEW

You and *GO!*

A project in which students use information from their own lives and apply the skills from the chapter to a personal task.

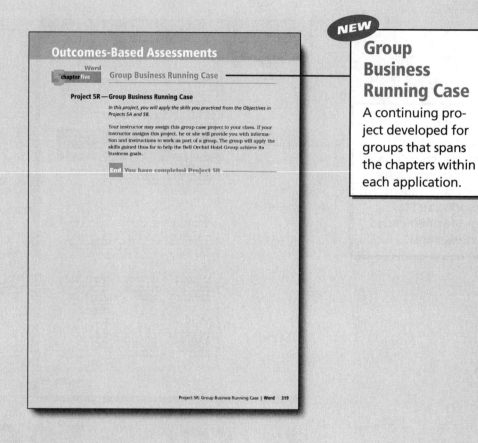

NEW

Group Business Running Case

A continuing project developed for groups that spans the chapters within each application.

Student CD includes:

- Student Data Files
- There's More You Can Do!
- Business Running Case
- You and *GO!*

Companion Web site

An interactive Web site to further student leaning.

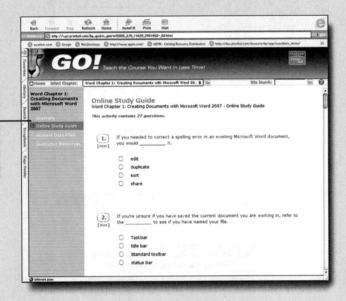

Online Study Guide

Interactive objective-style questions to help students study.

Annotated Instructor Edition

The Annotated Instructor Edition contains a full version of the student textbook that includes tips, supplement references, and pointers on teaching with the *GO!* instructional system.

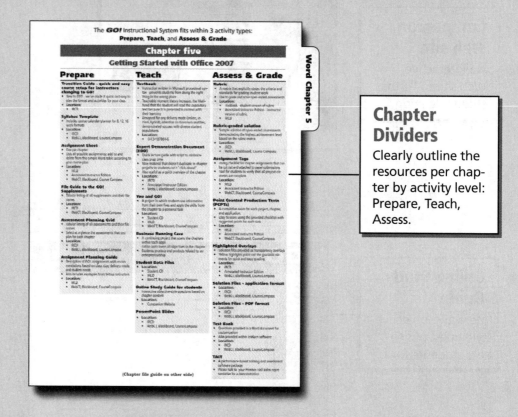

Chapter Dividers

Clearly outline the resources per chapter by activity level: Prepare, Teach, Assess.

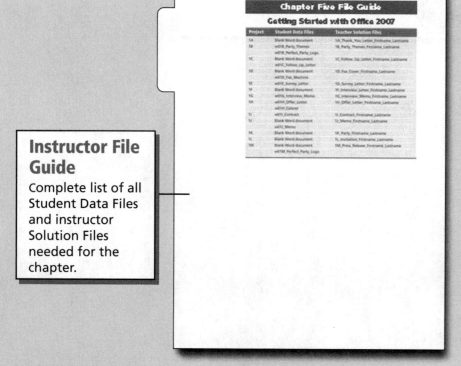

Instructor File Guide

Complete list of all Student Data Files and instructor Solution Files needed for the chapter.

Helpful Hints, Teaching Tips, Expand the Project

References correspond to what is being taught in the student textbook.

Full-Size Textbook Pages

An instructor copy of the textbook with traditional Instructor Manual content incorporated.

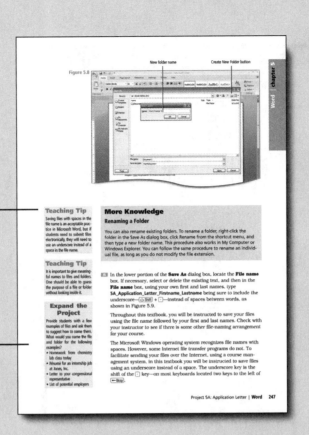

End-of-Chapter Concepts Assessments

Contain the answers for quick reference.

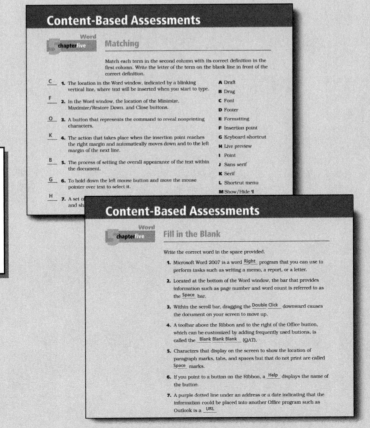

NEW

Rubric

A matrix to guide the student on how they will be assessed is reprinted in the Annotated Instructor Edition with suggested weights for each of the criteria and levels of performance. Instructors can modify the weights to suit their needs.

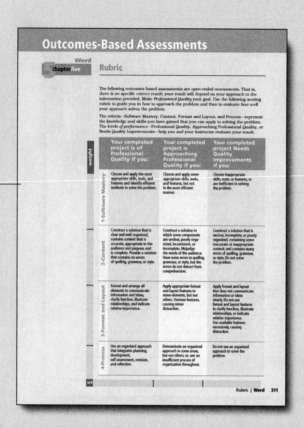

Assignment Tags

NEW

Scoring checklist for assignments. Now also available for Problem-Solving projects.

GO! with Microsoft® Office 2007

Assignment Tags for GO! with Office 2007
Word Chapter 5

Name:	Project:	5A	Name:	Project:	5B
Professor:	Course:		Professor:	Course:	
Task	Points	Your Score	Task	Points	Your Score
Center text vertically on page	2		Insert the file w05B_Music_School_Records	4	
Delete the word "really"	1		Insert the Music Logo	4	
Delete the words "try to"	1		Remove duplicate "and"	2	
Replace "last" with "first"	1		Change spelling and grammar errors (4)	8	
Insert the word "potential"	1		Correct/Add footer as instructed	2	
Replace "John W. Diamond" with "Lucy Burrows"	2		Circled information is incorrect or formatted incorrectly		
Change entire document to the Cambria font	2				
Change the first line of text to Arial Black 20 pt. font	2				
Bold the first line of text	2				
Change the 2nd through 4th lines to Arial 10 pt.	2				
Italicize the 2nd through 4th lines of text	2				
Correct/Add footer as instructed	2				
Circled information is incorrect or formatted incorrectly					
Total Points	**20**	**0**	**Total Points**	**20**	**0**
Name:	Project:	5C	Name:	Project:	5D
Professor:	Course:		Professor:	Course:	
Task	Points	Your Score	Task	Points	Your Score
Add four line letterhead	2		Insert the file w05D_Marketing	4	
Insert today's date	1		Bold the first two title lines	2	
Add address block, subject line, and greeting	2		Correct spelling of "Marketting"	2	
Add two-paragraph body of letter	2		Correct spelling of "geners"	2	
Add closing, name, and title	2		Correct all misspellings of "allready"	2	
In subject line, capitalize "receipt"	1		Correct grammar error "are" to "is"	2	
Change "standards" to "guidelines"	1		Insert the Piano image	4	
Insert "quite"	1		Correct/add footer as instructed	2	
Insert "all"	1		Circled information is incorrect or formatted incorrectly		
Change the first line of text to Arial Black 20 pt. font	2				
Bold the first line of text	1				
Change the 2nd through 4th lines to Arial 10 pt.	1				
Italicize the 2nd through 4th lines of text	1				
Correct/add footer as instructed	2				
Circled information is incorrect or formatted incorrectly					
Total Points	**20**	**0**	**Total Points**	**20**	**0**

Highlighted Overlays

Solution files provided as transparency overlays. Yellow highlights point out the gradable elements for quick and easy grading.

Music School Records
[20 point Arial Black, bold and underline]

2620 Vine Street
Los Angeles, CA 90028 *[10 point Arial, italic]*
323-555-0028

September 12, 2009

Mr. William Hawken
123 Eighth Street
Harrisville, MI 48740

[Text vertically centered on page]

[Body of document changed to Cambria font, 11 point]

Dear William:

Subject: Your Application to Music School Records

Thank you for submitting your application to Music School Records. Our talent scout for Northern Michigan, Catherine McDonald, is very enthusiastic about your music, and the demo CD you submitted certainly confirms her opinion. *[Word "really" deleted]*

We discuss our applications from potential clients during the first week of each month. We will have a decision for you by the second week of October. *[Words "try to" deleted]*

Yours Truly,

Lucy Burroughs

Point-Counted Production Tests (PCPTs)

A cumulative exam for each **project**, **chapter**, and **application**. Easy to score using the provided checklist with suggested points for each task.

GO! with Microsoft® Office 2007 Introductory

Point-Counted Production Test—Project for GO! with Microsoft® Office 2007 Introductory Project 5A

Instructor Name: _____

Course Information: _____

1. Start Word 2007 to begin a new blank document. Save your document as 5A_Cover_Letter_Firstname_Lastname Remember to save your file frequently as you work.

2. If necessary, display the formatting marks. With the insertion point blinking in the upper left corner of the document to the left of the default first paragraph mark, type the current date (you can use AutoComplete).

3. Press Enter three times and type the inside address:

   Music School Records
   2620 Vine Street
   Los Angeles, CA 90028

4. Press Enter three times, and type Dear Ms. Burroughs:

   Press Enter twice, and type Subject: Application to Music School Records

   Press Enter twice, and type the following text (skipping one line between paragraphs):

   I read about Music School Records in Con Brio magazine and I would like to inquire about the possibility of being represented by your company.

   I am very interested in a career in jazz and am planning to relocate to the Los Angeles area in the very near future. I would be interested in learning more about the company and about available opportunities.

   I was a member of my high school jazz band for three years. In addition, I have been playing in the local coffee shop for the last two years. My demo CD, which is enclosed, contains three of my most requested songs.

   I would appreciate the opportunity to speak with you. Thank you for your time and consideration. I look forward to speaking with you about this exciting opportunity.

5. Press Enter three times, and type the closing Sincerely, Press enter four times, and type your name.

6. Insert a footer that contains the file name.

7. Delete the first instance of the word *very* in the second body paragraph, and insert the word modern in front of *jazz*.

Copyright © 2008 Pearson Prentice Hall   Page 1 of 1

Test Bank

Available as TestGen Software or as a Word document for customization.

Chapter 5: Creating Documents with Microsoft Word 2007

Multiple Choice:

1. With word processing programs, how are documents stored?

   A. On a network

   B. On the computer

   C. Electronically

   D. On the floppy disk

   Answer: C   **Reference:** Objective 1: Create and Save a New Document   **Difficulty:** Moderate

2. Because you will see the document as it will print, _____ view is the ideal view to use when learning Microsoft Word 2007.

   A. Reading

   B. Normal

   C. Print Layout

   D. Outline

   Answer: C   **Reference:** Objective 1: Create and Save a New Document   **Difficulty:** Moderate

3. The blinking vertical line where text or graphics will be inserted is called the:

   A. cursor.

   B. insertion point.

   C. blinking line.

   D. I-beam.

   Answer: B   **Reference:** Objective 1: Create and Save a New Document   **Difficulty:** Easy

**Solution Files–
Application
and PDF
format**

Music School Records

Music School Records discovers, launches, and develops the careers of young artists in classical, jazz, and contemporary music. Our philosophy is to not only shape, distribute, and sell a music product, but to help artists create a career that can last a lifetime. Too often in the music industry, artists are forced to fit their music to a trend that is short-lived. Music School Records does not just follow trends, we take a long-term view of the music industry and help our artists develop a style and repertoire that is fluid and flexible and that will appeal to audiences for years and even decades.

The music industry is constantly changing, but over the last decade, the changes have been enormous. New forms of entertainment such as DVDs, video games, and the Internet mean there is more competition for the leisure dollar in the market. New technologies give consumers more options for buying and listening to music, and they are demanding high quality recordings. Young consumers are comfortable with technology and want the music they love when and where they want it, no matter where they are or what they are doing.

Music School Records embraces new technologies and the sophisticated market of young music lovers. We believe that providing high quality recordings of truly talented artists make for more discerning listeners who will cherish the gift of music for the rest of their lives. The expertise of Music School Records includes:

- Insight into our target market and the ability to reach the desired audience
- The ability to access all current sources of music income
- A management team with years of experience in music commerce
- Innovative business strategies and artist development plans
- Investment in technology infrastructure for high quality recordings and business services

pagexxxix_top.docx

Online Assessment and Training

my**it**lab is Prentice Hall's new performance-based solution that allows you to easily deliver outcomes-based courses on Microsoft Office 2007, with customized training and defensible assessment. Key features of my**it**lab include:

A *true* "system" approach: my**it**lab content is the same as in your textbook.
Project-based *and* skills-based: Students complete real-life assignments.
Advanced reporting *and* gradebook: These include student click stream data.
***No* installation required:** my**it**lab is completely Web-based. You just need an Internet connection, small plug-in, and Adobe Flash Player.

Ask your Prentice Hall sales representative for a demonstration or visit:

www.prenhall.com/myitlab

chapterone

Getting Started with Internet Explorer 7.0

OBJECTIVES

At the end of this chapter you will be able to:

1. Start Internet Explorer 7.0 and Identify Screen Elements
2. Navigate the Internet
3. Create and Manage Favorites
4. Search the Internet
5. Save and Print Web Pages

OUTCOMES

Mastering these objectives will enable you to:

PROJECT 1A

Use Internet Explorer 7.0 to Navigate and Search the Internet, Create and Manage Favorite Internet Sites, and Save and Print Web Pages.

Lake Michigan City College

Lake Michigan City College is located along the lakefront of Chicago—one of the nation's most exciting cities. The college serves its large and diverse student body and makes positive contributions to the community through relevant curricula, partnerships with businesses and nonprofit organizations, and learning experiences that allow students to be full participants in the global community. The college offers three associate degrees in 20 academic areas, adult education programs, and continuing education offerings on campus, at satellite locations, and online.

Getting Started with Internet Explorer 7.0

The Internet got its start in the 1960s as an experiment by the Department of Defense as a way for large computers to communicate with other large computers. The Internet has evolved into the largest online computer network in the world—one accessed by hundreds of millions of people every day.

Today, using the Internet, you are able to locate old classmates, communicate with friends by using e-mail or chat, or find phone numbers, directions, and maps so you can arrange visits. The Internet allows you to explore the museums of the world or shop for items that are unavailable at your local mall, all with a click of a button. You can control your finances or improve your mind with educational opportunities any time of day and from any location. The Internet gives you a greater connection to the world.

This introduction to Internet Explorer 7.0 provides a basic overview of Internet Explorer features and how to use them to explore the Internet. You will practice accessing Web sites, navigating the Internet, saving your favorite Web sites, searching for information, and saving and printing Web pages.

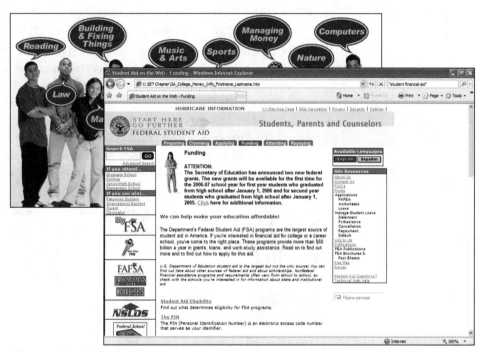

Project 1A College and Career Information

In Activities 1.1 through 1.15, you and the students in Mr. Tony Adair's CIS 101 course will use Internet Explorer 7.0 to find information about opportunities after graduating from Lake Michigan City College. Some students are interested in transferring to a four-year college and others want to begin a job and work for awhile before thinking about more college. Your completed projects will look similar, but not identical, to those shown in Figure 1.1.

For Project 1A, you will need the following file:

New blank document

You will save your files as
1A_College_Money_Info_Firstname_Lastname
1A_Career_Info_Firstname_Lastname

Figure 1.1
Project 1A—College and Career Information

Objective 1
Start Internet Explorer 7.0 and Identify Screen Elements

Internet Explorer 7.0 is a software program that allows you to view the contents of the World Wide Web. Software of this type is called a *Web browser*. By using Internet Explorer as your Web browser, you can connect to the Internet to search for information, display Web pages, and receive e-mail. Internet Explorer also assists with downloading and transferring files from the Internet, displaying the graphics on a Web site, playing audio and video files associated with a Web site, and executing small programs found in Web sites.

Activity 1.1 Starting Internet Explorer

In the following activity, you will start Internet Explorer 7.0 and identify features of the Internet Explorer program window. The way you start Internet Explorer will vary depending on the version of Windows you are using and the way your system has been set up by you, your college, or your organization. The standard installation of Windows places Internet Explorer at the top of the Start menu.

1 On the Windows taskbar, click the **Start** button [start], and then using Figure 1.2 as a guide, locate Internet Explorer on your system.

Organizations can customize the arrangement of programs on the Start menu. If Internet Explorer is used as the standard browser program on your computer, it displays at the top of the Start menu along with the standard e-mail program—Microsoft Office Outlook. In other cases, Internet Explorer will display in the All Programs list. If the Internet Explorer logo displays as an icon on your desktop, you can double-click the desktop icon to start the program. The Internet Explorer logo may also display on the Quick Launch toolbar.

Figure 1.2

Internet Explorer icon on the desktop

Internet Explorer on the Start menu

Internet Explorer on the All Programs menu

Are you sure that you have an Internet connection?

To complete the activities in this chapter, your system must be connected to the Internet. This connection may be through your college or organization's network or your personal *Internet Service Provider (ISP)*. An Internet Service Provider is a company that provides an Internet connection through a regular telephone line, a special high-speed telephone line, or a cable. These services are provided by companies such as AOL or Earthlink, or by local cable and telephone companies.

2 On your system, click **Internet Explorer**. In the upper right corner, **Maximize** 🗗 the window if it is not already maximized.

Each time you start Internet Explorer when you are connected to the Internet, the home page that has been set on your system displays. Your *home page* is the Web page that displays every time you start Internet Explorer and can be any Web page. In a college environment, the home page is usually set to the college's home page. On your own system you can choose any page. The default home page for Internet Explorer 7.0 is the Microsoft Web page.

A *Web page* is a document on the World Wide Web that displays as a screen with associated links, frames, pictures, and other features of interest. A *Web site* is a group of related Web pages published to a specific location on the World Wide Web; for example, all the various screens—pages—that comprise your college's Web site. Each Web site has its own unique address, called a *Uniform Resource Locator* or *URL*.

3 In the address bar, type **MSN.com**, and then press Enter. Because a Web address is not case sensitive, it does not matter whether you use lowercase, uppercase, or a combination of uppercase and lowercase letters when typing the address. Compare your screen with Figure 1.3.

Your screen may look slightly different than Figure 1.3.

Figure 1.3

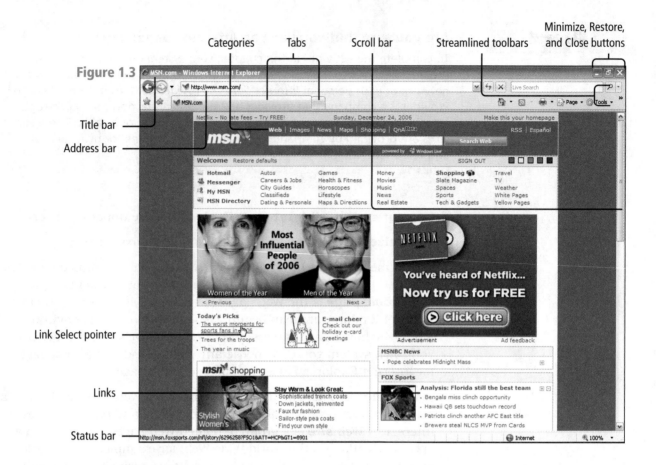

Categories Tabs Scroll bar Streamlined toolbars Minimize, Restore, and Close buttons

Title bar

Address bar

Link Select pointer

Links

Status bar

4 Click the **Add to Favorites** button 🗝, and then click **Add to Favorites** to display the **Add a Favorite** dialog box. Compare your screen with Figure 1.4.

Figure 1.4

Add to Favorites button

Add a Favorite dialog box

Web site name to be added to Favorites

Add button

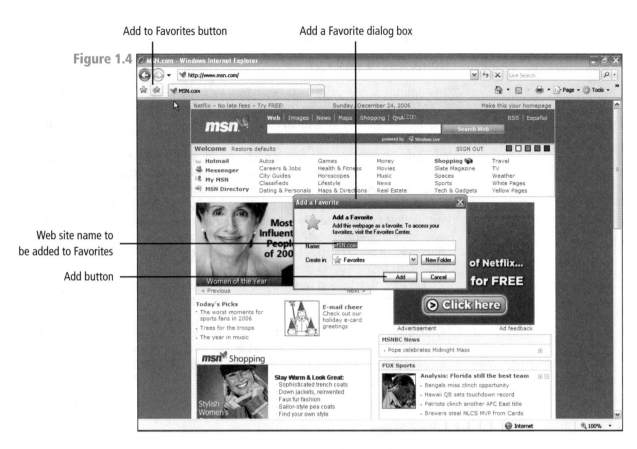

5 In the **Add a Favorite** dialog box, click the **Add** button. Take a moment to review Figure 1.3 and the table in Figure 1.5.

Recall that because Web sites are regularly updated, your screen will differ from Figure 1.3.

Microsoft Internet Explorer Screen Elements

Screen Element	Description
Title bar	Identifies the program as Windows Internet Explorer and also displays the name of the active Web page.
Minimize, Restore, and Close buttons	Provide a way to vary the size of the screen you are viewing.
Toolbar	Contains buttons for some of the most common commands in Internet Explorer.
Address bar	Displays the address of the active Web page.
Categories	Link you to other main pages in the Web site; this arrangement varies from site to site.
Mouse pointer	Displays as a pointing hand when you point to a link (Link Select pointer).
Links	When clicked, display other Web pages in this site, or other Web sites. Links can also take you to a document, e-mail address, picture, or sound clip.
Scroll bar	Allows vertical or horizontal navigation of a Web page.
Status bar	Provides information about the security of a site and information about a link's destination as you point to a link.
Tabs	Allow multiple Web sites to be open at the same time.

Figure 1.5

More Knowledge

Home Pages and Portals

The default home page installed when Windows is set up on your computer is a Microsoft site because Internet Explorer is a Microsoft program. Schools, organizations, and individuals that have Web sites often change the default settings to display their own site as the home page. As part of the installation process, ISPs such as AOL and Earthlink and sites such as eBay and Yahoo! offer to change the home page to their Web sites to make accessing e-mail and other frequently used features easier. These home pages, including MSN, act as *portals* or launching sites to other Web pages. They contain links to frequently visited sites, up-to-the-minute news, weather reports, maps, and directories. The portal pages are also customizable so that you can replace the standard links and information presented on the page with features you use.

On school, lab, and business computers, changing the home page is usually not recommended. However, on your personal computer, you can change the home page. To do so, display the page you want to set as the home page. Then, on the toolbar, click the Home down arrow and select Add or Change Home Page. In the Add or Change Home Page dialog box, review the choices, click one of the option buttons, and then click Yes.

Objective 2
Navigate the Internet

Most Web pages contain links that you can use to navigate to other sites on the Internet. Internet Explorer also provides commands that are accessible on the toolbars, a History list, and the Address bar, all of which you can use to navigate the Web. Internet Explorer has tabs that allow you to have multiple Web sites open at the same time. In Activities 1.2 through 1.6, you will use each of these tools to access different Web sites.

Activity 1.2 Performing Commands Using the Toolbar

1 Click the **Back** button ⬅ to return to your home page, and then notice that the **Forward** button ➡ becomes available.

2 On the toolbar, point to, but do not click, the **Forward** button ➡, and then compare your screen with Figure 1.6.

A ScreenTip identifies the Web page that will display when you click the button.

A *ScreenTip* is a small note that displays information about a screen element and is activated by pointing to a button or other screen object.

Forward button   Home button   Refresh button   Stop button

Figure 1.6
Back button

ScreenTip

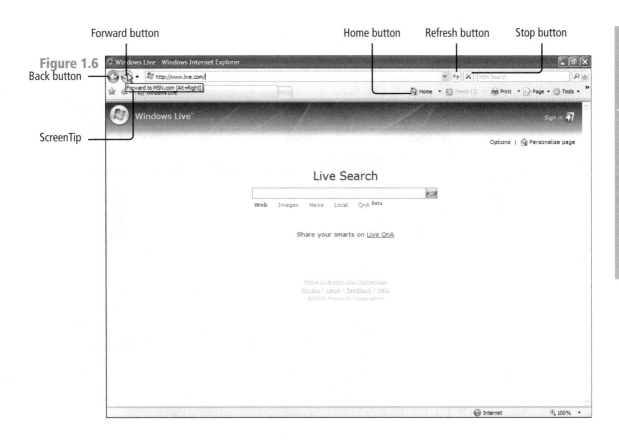

3 On the toolbar, click the **Forward** button ⊙ to redisplay the *MSN.com* home page.

4 On the toolbar, click the **Home** button.

Regardless of how many Web pages you view or Web sites you visit, clicking the Home button returns you to the site that is set as the home page on the system at which you are working.

Activity 1.3 Accessing Web Sites from the Address Bar

1 Near the top of the Internet Explorer window, click anywhere in the **Address Bar** box.

The existing Web address is highlighted indicating that it is selected.

2 With the current Web address selected, type **www.firstgov.gov** Press ⏎, and then compare your screen with Figure 1.7.

The FirstGov.gov site's home page displays. When an existing Web address is selected, typing a new address replaces the selected text. As you type, a list may display. Internet Explorer remembers the last 25 Web addresses you entered and displays a list containing site addresses that start with the characters you type. When you type *www*, Internet Explorer displays a list of all the sites you have accessed recently that begin with *www*. The list gets shorter with each character you type. If you see the site you are typing in the Address Bar list, you can click the site name in the list rather than typing the complete address.

Figure 1.7

Home page of the *FirstGov.gov* Web site (your screen will likely differ)

3 Take a moment to study the table in Figure 1.8 that describes how Web addresses are formed.

Parts of a Web Address

Part of the Web Address	Description
http	The abbreviation of Hypertext Transfer Protocol—the standard *protocol* for retrieving Web sites. Another protocol is *ftp*, or *File Transfer Protocol*. A protocol is a set of rules for transferring data over the Internet.
://	Three characters identified by Internet creators for separating the protocol from the rest of the Web address. These three characters were identified because they had never appeared together in computer programs and other computer-related contexts.
www.firstgov.gov	The domain name. In this case, the domain name includes the abbreviation for World Wide Web *(www)*, the name of the organization, and the domain type—*.gov* stands for government. Not all domain names start with www, but many do. Other domain types include *.com* (commercial), *.edu* (education), *.org* (organization), *.net* (network), *.mil* (military), and *.mus* (music). Most countries have their own domain types such as .ca for Canada and .fr for France.

Figure 1.8

4 Click the **Address Bar** box again, type **www.bls.gov** and press Enter. Compare your screen with Figure 1.9.

The U.S. Department of Labor, Bureau of Labor Statistics Web site displays. Recall that because sites are regularly updated, your screen will likely not match Figure 1.9 exactly. The *.gov* in the Web address is called a top-level domain and identifies the site as a government site.

Web address

U.S. Department of Labor,
Bureau of Labor Statistics Web site

Figure 1.9

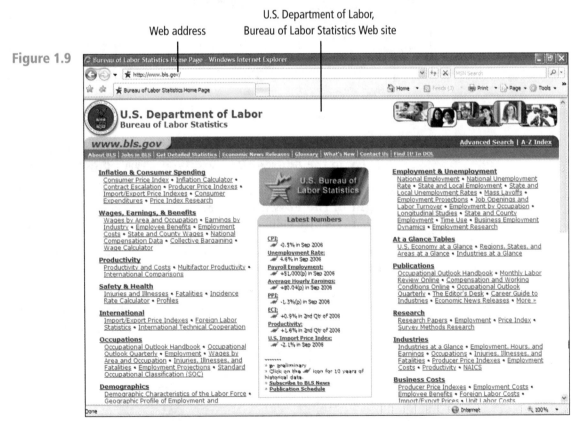

5 At the right end of the **Address Bar** box, click the **Address Bar box down arrow** and point to, but do not click, the **http://www.firstgov.gov** Web address. Compare your screen with Figure 1.10.

The list of recently accessed Web sites on your computer will differ from those shown in Figure 1.10. The sites listed represent those most frequently visited on your system.

Site to select   Address Bar box down arrow

Figure 1.10

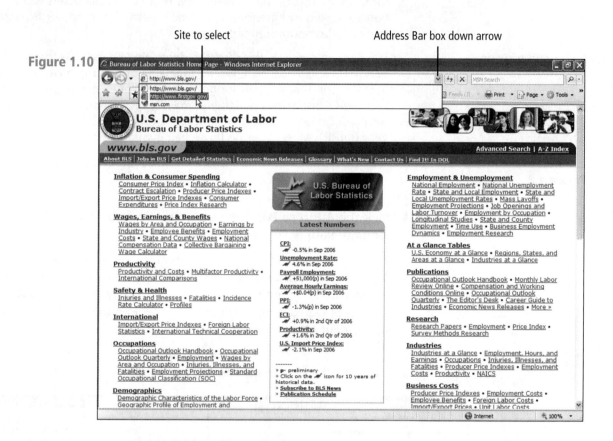

6 In the displayed list, click the **http://www.firstgov.gov** Web address. Then, in the **Address Bar** box, type **www.ed.gov** and press Enter.

7 On the toolbar, locate the **Recent Pages button down arrow to the right of the Forward button**, and then click the arrow to display the most recently visited Web sites. Click the listing for the **FirstGov.gov** Web site. Then, click the **Forward** button to return to the **U.S. Department of Education** Web site. Compare your screen with Figure 1.11.

The U.S. Department of Education Web site displays, and the Forward button is unavailable because you have used it to return to this Web site.

Recent Pages button
down arrow

Figure 1.11

Forward button (which is
unavailable because you
used it to get to this site)

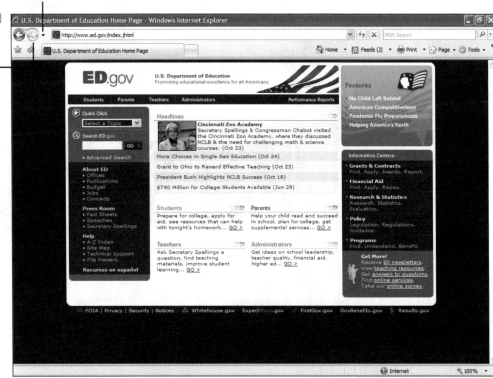

8 On the toolbar, click the **Favorites Center** button to display the task pane. Click **MSN.com**, and watch this site's home page for a few moments and notice that text and images change.

The **Favorites Center** allows you to view the Favorites, Feeds, and History lists. Web sites frequently use **animated banners** to attract attention and stimulate interest to the Web site. Animated banners are a series of rotating or changing text and images embedded within the Web page. Compare your screen with Figure 1.12.

Site address

Figure 1.12

Animated banner

9 In the **Address Bar** box, type **www.psu.edu** and press Enter. Compare your screen with Figure 1.13.

Internet Explorer displays the Penn State Web site. The *.edu* extension is reserved for schools, colleges, and universities.

Figure 1.13

Activity 1.4 Opening a Second Web Site

1 On the right of the **Welcome to Penn State's Home on the Web** tab, position your mouse pointer over the **New Tab**, but do not click. Compare your screen with Figure 1.14.

A ScreenTip displays indicating a new tab will be opened.

Tabs in Internet Explorer 7.0 allow you to have multiple Web pages open at the same time without having to open multiple browsers.

ScreenTip

Figure 1.14

New Tab

2 Click **New Tab.**

A new tab displays that allows you to view another Web site while keeping the Penn State Web site open.

3 In the **Address Bar** box, type the Web site of your school, and then press [Enter]. Compare your screen with Figure 1.15.

Your school's Web site displays and the name of the Web page displays on the new tab along with a Close button.

Figure 1.15

Your school's Web
site in new tab   Close tab button

4 Use the **Close tab** button ☒ to close the tab displaying your
school's Web page.

5 On the toolbar, click the **Home** button to return to the home page
that is set on your computer.

Activity 1.5 Displaying Web Pages with Hyperlinks

Most Web sites contain *hyperlinks*, which provide another navigation
tool for browsing Web pages. Hyperlinks are text, buttons, pictures, or
other objects displayed on Web pages that, when clicked, access other
Web pages or display other sections of the active page. Linked Web pages
can be pages within the same Web site or Web pages on sites of other
companies, schools, or organizations. In this activity, you will use hyperlinks to display Web pages about college financial aid.

1 In the **Address Bar** box, type **www.students.gov** and then press Enter.
Move the mouse pointer to various parts of the screen to locate

areas where the **Link Select pointer** 🖑 displays, as shown in
Figure 1.16.

Internet Explorer displays the students.gov home page. As you
review Figure 1.16, notice that the mouse pointer displays as a
pointing hand—the *Link Select pointer*—when you point to an item
that links to another Web page. Many Web pages contain links that
connect to other pages on the site. These other pages contain links
that lead back to the home page.

Figure 1.16

Scholarships & grants link ——

Link Select pointer ——

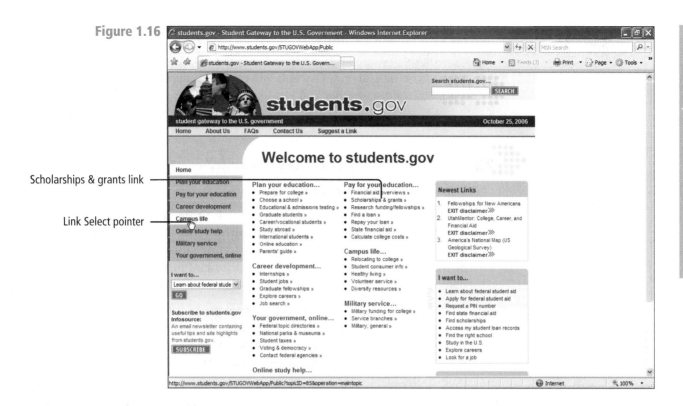

2 Locate and then click the link for **Scholarships & grants**. Compare your screen with Figure 1.17.

The Scholarships & grants screen displays. The address in the Address bar still shows the *students.gov* Web site, but the URL has expanded to identify the path for this page.

Expanded URL path

Figure 1.17

Students.gov Home link ——

Scholarships & grants page title ——

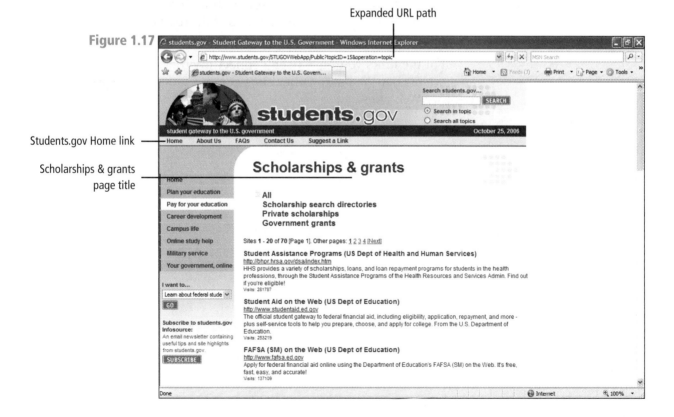

3 On the toolbar, click the **Back** button ⬅.

The students.gov home page displays.

4 Scroll down as necessary to locate the link for **State financial aid** and click it. Compare your screen with Figure 1.18. Click on your state to try to find information about your state's financial aid. One or more links to information about financial aid in your state will display below the list of states. Click any one of these links.

Internet Explorer opens the individual state's financial aid links in a new window. Each Web page contains settings that control whether linked pages open in a separate window or in the same window. In addition, settings that are active on your computer control the linked page's display.

The new Web page opens in a separate window because the window displays as a *pop-up* on top of the State financial aid window. Pop-ups are sometimes distracting windows that display on your screen without you actually requesting them. Many Web users use a *pop-up blocker* to stop these unwanted windows from displaying. Pop-up windows that are launched when the user clicks a link usually will not be blocked. Notice that another button displays on the Windows taskbar at the bottom of your screen that shows the name of the new Web page. Both the Back and Forward buttons of the new window are unavailable.

All of the links you have used connect to other pages within the *students.gov* Web site. Other sites contain links that connect you to other Web sites.

Figure 1.18

⑤ When you are finished viewing the information, return to the State financial aid Web page by clicking the **Close** button ⊠ in the upper right corner of the new window.

⑥ Click in the **Address Bar** box, type **www.usgovernment.com** and press Enter. Compare your screen with Figure 1.19.

Figure 1.19

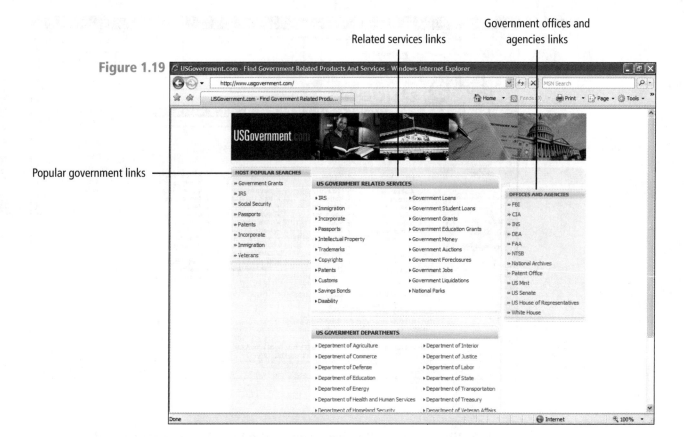

Related services links

Government offices and agencies links

Popular government links

7 Locate and then click the link for **Government Education Grants**. Scroll down if necessary, and click the link to **www.freewebs.com**. Compare your screen with Figure 1.20. The new window that opens may differ from the one shown here. Notice that the top-level domain name (*.com*) in the Address bar is a commercial Web site. It has paid to be listed prominently in the search returns.

Internet Explorer opens each of the links shown on the Government Education Grants Web page in a new window. You can see that the new Web page opens in a separate window because the window displays as a pop-up on top of the Government Education Grants window and another button displays on the Windows taskbar at the bottom of your screen that shows the name of the new Web page. Both the Back and Forward buttons of the new window are unavailable.

Unavailable Back and
Forward buttons

Link opened in new window

Figure 1.20

Sponsored Results for
Government Education Grants

New window's button on
the Windows taskbar

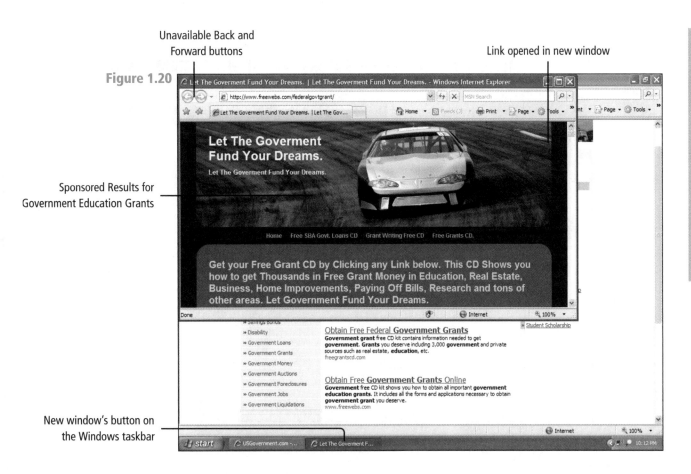

8 On the displayed Web site's title bar, click the **Close** button ☒ to close the new window. Then click the **Home** button to return to your home page.

Activity 1.6 Using Internet Explorer History

The Internet Explorer *History* feature tracks recently visited Web pages and sites. You can display the History list by using the Favorites Center button, and then choosing a site that you recently visited. By default, Internet Explorer tracks sites visited in the last 20 days. To reduce the amount of disk storage space required to maintain the History list, you can customize the settings to change the number of days tracked and to clear the list. In this activity, you will use the History list to display recently visited sites.

1 On the toolbar, click the **Favorites Center** button ⭐, click the down arrow on the **History** button, click **By Date**, and then click **Today**. Compare your screen with Figure 1.21.

The History list displays on the left side of the Internet Explorer window. The listings of items on your computer will differ from those shown in the figure. However, many of the listings shown for Today should be the same. Notice that the links to sites accessed today display in alphabetical order.

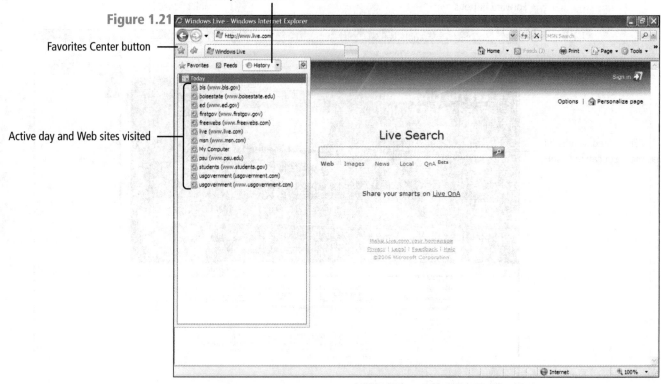

Figure 1.21

History button and down arrow

Favorites Center button

Active day and Web sites visited

2 In the **History** list, click the **bls (www.bls.gov)** link, and then compare your screen with Figure 1.22.

The Web site name associated with the folder displays as a link below the folder. If you click the link, the Web site will open. This is another way to load a Web site link into a window.

bls (www.bls.gov) link

Figure 1.22

Associated Web site

Scroll down the **History** list as necessary, and then click the **firstgov** link to display the associated Web site name for the Firstgov.gov Web site. Click on the link to open the **Firstgov.gov** Web site.

More Knowledge

Setting History Options

The default setting for the History list displays Web pages visited in the last 20 days. You can change the options that control and clear the History list by setting Internet Options. On the Internet Explorer toolbar, click the Tools button, and then click Internet Options to open the Internet Options dialog box. In the dialog box under Browsing History, click the Delete button to open the Delete Browsing History dialog box. Click the Delete history button to remove all site listings; then click Yes to confirm the deletion. Click the Close button to return to the Internet Options dialog box. To change the number of days tracked on the History list, under Browsing History, click the Settings button. Toward the bottom of the Temporary Internet Files and History Settings dialog box, click the spin arrows beside *Days to keep pages in history* to increase or decrease the number of days tracked on the History list. Click OK two times to return to the Web page.

Objective 3
Create and Manage Favorites

The History list automatically tracks sites that you visit each time you start Internet Explorer—many of which you may never visit again. The Favorites list works differently. The Favorites list contains Web addresses for sites you plan to visit frequently. You intentionally add addresses to the Favorites list and Internet Explorer keeps the list for you. When you install Internet Explorer, a short list of Microsoft sites is added to the Favorites list. You can delete these addresses, add new addresses, and organize favorite site addresses into folders. For example, you may have a folder for Travel Sites, for College Sites, and so on. In Activities 1.7 through 1.9, you will add a new favorite, create a new folder, navigate to a site listed in the favorites, and delete a favorite.

Activity 1.7 Adding an Address to the Favorites List

In this activity, you will display a Web page and add it to the Favorites list, using the Add Favorite button.

1 In the **Address Bar** box, type **www.prenhall.com/go** and then press Enter.

2 On the toolbar, click the **Add to Favorites** button, and then click **Add to Favorites** to display the **Add a Favorite** dialog box. Compare your screen with Figure 1.23.

The Add a Favorite dialog box displays with the name of the Web site indicated in the Name box.

Name of Web page

Figure 1.23

Add to Favorites button

Add button

3 In the **Add a Favorite** dialog box, click **Add**.

4 On the toolbar, click the **Add to Favorites** button 🌟, and then click **Organize Favorites**. In the **Organize Favorites** dialog box, click the **New Folder** button. In the new folder that was added to the list, type **Textbook Sites** and then press Enter.

The folder is created and displays in the listing of all folders and Web site favorites that are already established. When you have a number of sites that are related to a specific topic, you can create a new folder and use it to store related site addresses.

5 In the **Organize Favorites** dialog box, click the **GO! bridge page,** and then click the **Move** command button. In the **Browse For Folder** dialog box, click the **Textbook Sites** folder, and then click **OK**. In the **Organize Favorites** dialog box, click the **Close** button.

Internet Explorer adds the Prentice Hall GO! Series Web page address to the folder in the Favorites list.

Another Way ── **To Move a Web Site to a Folder**

After the folder is created, in the Organize Favorites dialog box, drag the Web site to the desired folder.

---

6 Click the **Home** button to display your home page.

Activity 1.8 Displaying a Favorite Web Site

In this activity, you will use the Favorites list to display a Web site.

1 On the toolbar, click the **Favorites Center** button ⭐. If necessary, click the **Favorites** button, click the **Textbook Sites** folder, and then notice that the link to the Prentice Hall GO! Series displays, as shown in Figure 1.24.

Figure 1.24

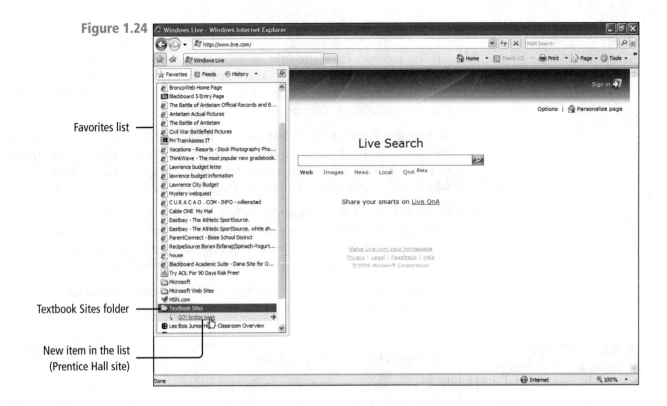

Favorites list

Textbook Sites folder

New item in the list
(Prentice Hall site)

2 Click the link to the **Prentice Hall GO!** site.

The GO! Series Web site displays.

Activity 1.9 Deleting a Web Address from Favorites

In this activity, you will remove an address from the Favorites list.

1 On the toolbar, click the **Add to Favorites** button , click **Organize Favorites**, and then compare your screen with Figure 1.25.

The Organize Favorites dialog box displays a list of folders and links contained in the Favorites list and command buttons for creating folders, renaming folders and links, moving links to folders, and deleting folders and links from Favorites.

Command buttons

Figure 1.25

List of folders and links in the Favorites list

In the **Organize Favorites** dialog box, scroll down if necessary, click the **Textbook Sites** folder to list its contents, and then click the **GO! bridge page** link one time to select it.

In the **Organize Favorites** dialog box, click the **Delete** button, and then compare your screen with Figure 1.26.

Confirm File Delete dialog box

Figure 1.26

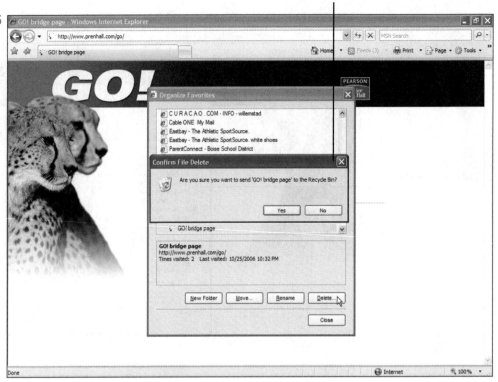

4 In the **Confirm File Delete** dialog box, click **Yes**, and then in the **Organize Favorites** dialog box, click **Close**.

Internet Explorer removes the Prentice Hall GO! Web site from the Favorites list and closes the Organize Favorites dialog box.

5 On the toolbar, click the **Home** button to display your home page.

Objective 4
Search the Internet

When you know the name of an organization or the Web address you want to locate, accessing the site is easy and straightforward. When you want to locate information about topics from a variety of sources, finding sites for businesses, journals, and other sources presents a greater challenge because of the large number of sites available on the Internet. There are several Web sites with search capabilities called *search engines*, programs that search for keywords in files and documents or other Web sites found on the Internet.

Internet Explorer includes an Instant Search box that connects to a default search engine (Windows Live) and easily allows you to add additional engines. In this activity, you will search the Internet for topics related to student financial aid.

Activity 1.10 Adding a Search Engine and Searching the Internet

1 On the toolbar, click the **Search Options down arrow** and then click **Find More Providers**.

A Web site opens that allows you to add additional search providers to Internet Explorer.

2 In the **Web Search** list, click **Google**, and in the **Add Search Provider** dialog box, click the **Make this my default search provider** check box. Compare your screen with Figure 1.27.

Add Provider button   Search Options down arrow

Figure 1.27

Google added as a search provider

Make Google the default search provider

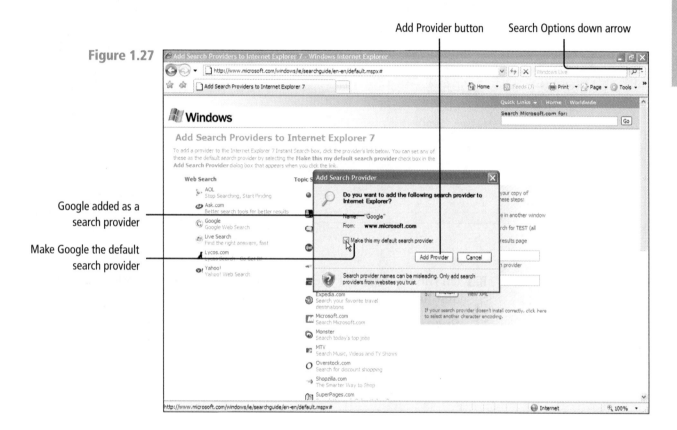

3 Click the **Add Provider** button.

4 On the toolbar in the **Search** box, type **"student financial aid"** including the quotation marks, and then press Enter. Compare your screen with Figure 1.28.

You can begin a search by typing a single word, a phrase, a question, or a statement. Typing *student financial aid* without the quotation marks directs the search engine to look for three different terms. Placing the text in quotation marks ensures that the search engine looks for sites that contain the entire phrase. You can see that the number of sites found during this particular search that contain the phrase *"student financial aid"* is quite large. Internet Explorer displays links to the Web sites in a ranked order based on the quality and quantity of the content at the Web sites it returns. Several factors are considered, such as how closely the site matches the search phrase, the number of references to the search text contained in the site, the number of other links to that site, and how recently the site has been updated.

Figure 1.28

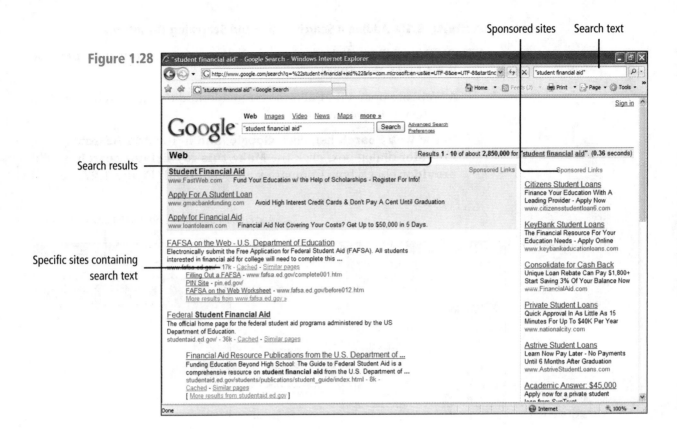

Search results

Specific sites containing
search text

⑤ On the right side of the screen, under **Sponsored Links**, click the
first link. Compare your screen with Figure 1.29.

Sponsored links are sites that pay to be displayed as results at a
search engine site. Sponsored links are frequently placed near the
top or on the right side of the search engine results page so they are
easily seen and clicked. Sponsored links generally are commercial
sites, so they stand to gain from increasing traffic to their Web site.

Web address of first sponsored site
(yours will vary)

Figure 1.29

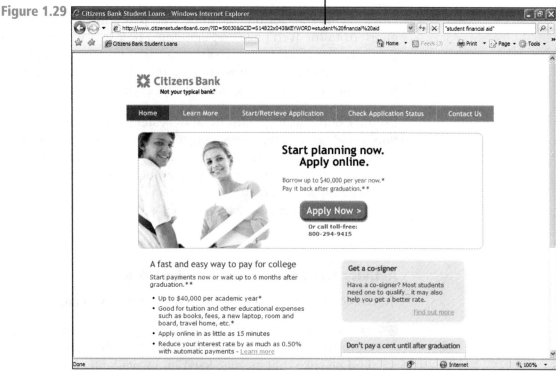

6 Click the **Back** button to return to your search results. Under **Web**, scroll as necessary, and then click the link for **Federal Student Financial Aid**.

The home page for student aid programs administered by the U.S. Department of Education displays. If you are interested in this information, you can print it or put it on your Favorites list to examine at a later time. Financial aid information found at sponsored Web sites is likely to be loan opportunities. Government financial aid Web sites are more likely to offer information on grant and scholarship opportunities.

7 On the toolbar, click the **Home** button to display your home page.

Objective 5
Save and Print Web Pages

Saving a copy of a Web page on your system or storage device is referred to as **downloading**. Downloading means that you request a copy of a file or program from a remote server, such as a Web server, and save it on your local system or storage device. You can also download other types of Web files, such as graphics, and save them on your computer or disk so that you can review them later. When you download a Web page displayed in Internet Explorer, Internet Explorer creates a new folder at the location you indicate to save all associated graphics, pictures, and other features of the Web page so that when you view the file offline, it resembles the entire page as it was displayed on the Web.

Other techniques for downloading Web pages include setting a desktop shortcut to the Web page and sending a link to a Web page to someone through e-mail. Setting a desktop shortcut creates an icon on your desktop for the downloaded Web page so that it opens very quickly. Both techniques are accomplished from the Page button.

Because of the widespread threat of system viruses, as a general precaution, avoid downloading or saving files from unknown Web sites, and be sure your virus protection program is up to date before storing Web files on your system. You must also be careful not to violate copyright-protected Web materials. Most materials found on the Web are copyrighted. It is illegal to download copyrighted materials without permission from the Web site owner.

Activity 1.11 Downloading and Saving a Web Page

In this activity, you will download and save a Web page.

1 Determine where you will be storing your files for this chapter, for example, on your own disk or USB flash drive, or on a network drive, and be sure that storage location is available. If necessary, check with your instructor or lab coordinator.

2 From the **Start** menu, click **My Computer**, and then navigate to the drive—USB flash drive, computer hard drive, or network drive—where you will be storing your files. Double-click the storage location to display the name of that drive on the title bar in the upper left corner of the window. From the **File** menu, point to **New**, and then click **Folder**. With **New Folder** selected, type **IE7 Chapter** and then press Enter. **Close** ☒ the window.

3 In **Internet Explorer**, in the **Address Bar** box, type **studentaid.ed.gov** and then press Enter. When the Federal Student Aid Web site displays, locate, and then click, the **Funding tab**.

4 On the toolbar, click the **Page** button, and then click **Save As**. In the displayed **Save Webpage** dialog box, click the **Save in arrow**, and then navigate to the drive, and then to your **IE7 Chapter** folder. Compare your screen with Figure 1.30.

Selected storage location (yours may vary)

Figure 1.30

Default file name

Default file type

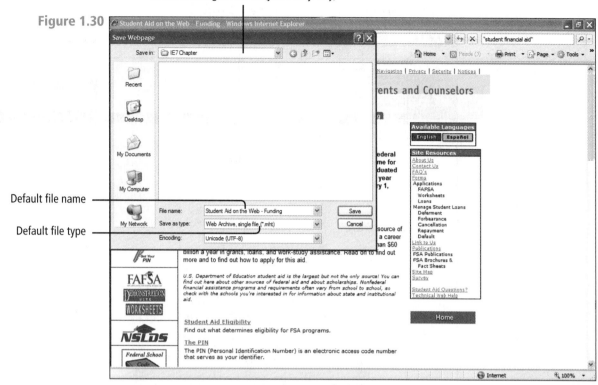

5. At the bottom of the **Save Webpage** dialog box, click the **Save as type arrow** and click **Webpage, complete**. Click in the **File name** box to select the existing text, and then replace the selected text by typing **1A_College_Money_Info_Firstname_Lastname** Be sure to use your own name for Firstname and Lastname, and instead of spaces between words, use the underscore key, which is ⌂Shift + -. Then, in the lower right corner, click the **Save** button.

6. Click the **Home** button. In the **Address** bar, type the drive, such as **c:** and the location where you saved the file, and the most recent files in that location will display. Compare your screen with Figure 1.31.

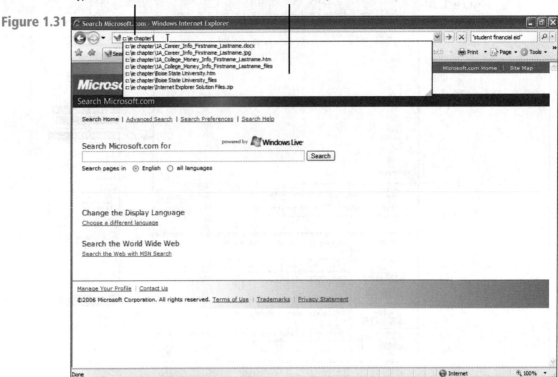

Type location in Address bar   Files recently saved to the
drive and directory

Figure 1.31

7 Scroll down as necessary, and click the file name that you saved in Step 5.

The Web page opens in Internet Explorer. Notice the Address bar shows the Web page address as the location where you saved the Web page. If you were looking at the actual Web page, the Address bar would display the URL as *http://studentaid.ed.gov/ PORTALSWebApp/students/english/funding.jsp?tab=funding*.

8 From the **Start** menu, open **My Computer** again, and then navigate to the drive where you stored the Web page.

You can see that Internet Explorer also created a folder to hold the files associated with the Student Aid on the Web page. Even though any given Web page looks as if it's one single file, it is actually made up of several objects and files. Each graphic is its own file and the text content is another file. The Web page may be divided into **frames** or separate areas of content placed closely together. The frames display all together as one Web page with or without any visible demarcation lines between them.

9 Double-click the **1A_College_Money_Info_Firstname_Lastname** folder to view the objects and files that are part of the Web file.

The folder keeps all of these files—graphics, text, and frames—together as one unit just as the browser displays them as one unit.

10 **Close** [X] the window displaying the files.

11 On the toolbar, click the **Home** button to display your home page.

More Knowledge

Downloading New Programs

Downloading, as you used it in Activity 1.11, saves a Web page and associated files in the folder you specify. You can also download entire software programs and other items from the Internet. For example, if you display the Microsoft.com Web site, you can download free trial programs, install them on your system, and try them before you purchase them. When sites offer free downloads, a **Download** link usually appears on the page. When you click the link, Internet Explorer prompts you to save the file on your system. The prompt message also provides an option to open or run the program from the server.

It is generally recommended that you download and save the file on your system before trying to install it. After it is saved to your system, run the program file through your virus scan software before installing the new program. A good rule to follow is to be careful what you download, and download only from well-known and trusted sites.

Activity 1.12 Downloading and Saving Graphics from a Web Page

1 In the **Address Bar** box, type **www.bls.gov** and then press Enter. On the Bureau of Labor Statistics Web site home page, scroll toward the bottom of the page, and then locate and click the **Career Information for Kids** link. Point anywhere in the displayed picture, right-click the mouse button to display a context-sensitive menu, and then click **Save Picture As**.

2 In the displayed **Save Picture** dialog box, click the **Save in arrow**, and then navigate to your **IE7 Chapter** folder so that its name displays in the **Save in** box. At the bottom of the dialog box, click in the **File name** box to select the existing text, and then replace it by typing **1A_Career_Info_Firstname_Lastname** Be sure to use your own first and last names and insert underscores between words instead of spaces. Compare your screen with Figure 1.32. Leave the **Save as type** box as the default type, and then in the lower right corner, click the **Save** button.

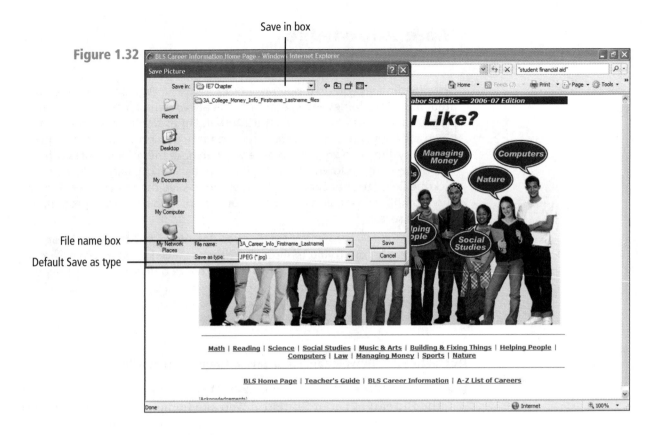

Figure 1.32

Save in box

File name box

Default Save as type

---

3 On the toolbar, click the **Home** button to display your home page.

Activity 1.13 Printing Web Pages

Web pages are constructed to contain a variety of different elements—pictures, navigation panes, links, text, and so on. When you print Web pages, all the elements displayed on the Web page print unless you select the specific text, picture, or frame you want to print. Most of the options contained in the Print dialog box in Internet Explorer are the same as those seen in the Print dialog box for other programs. However, the Print dialog box in Internet Explorer contains options that enable you to print pages, or a table of pages, that are linked to the active Web page.

Because frames and objects are placed so closely together on the Web page, selecting just the information you want to print can be a challenge without activating a hyperlink or selecting additional information as well. In this activity, you will review options in the Print dialog box and print a Web page.

1 From the **Start** menu, click **My Computer**, and then navigate to the drive—USB flash drive, computer hard drive, or network drive—where you stored your files. Locate and then double-click your HTML file—not the folder—**1A_College_Money_Info_Firstname_Lastname**. Compare your screen with Figure 1.33.

Figure 1.33

The Web site has been opened from a storage location

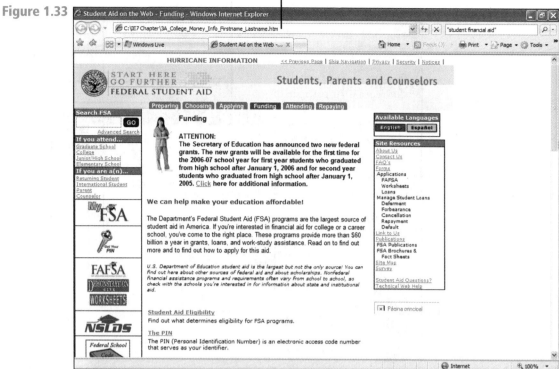

2 On the toolbar, click the **Print button down arrow**, and then click **Page Setup** to display the **Page Setup** dialog box. Under **Headers and Footers**, delete any information in the **Header** box. Then delete any information in the **Footer** box. In the **Footer** box, type **1A_College_Money_Info_Firstname_Lastname** and then compare your screen with Figure 1.34.

Page Setup dialog box   Footer box

Figure 1.34

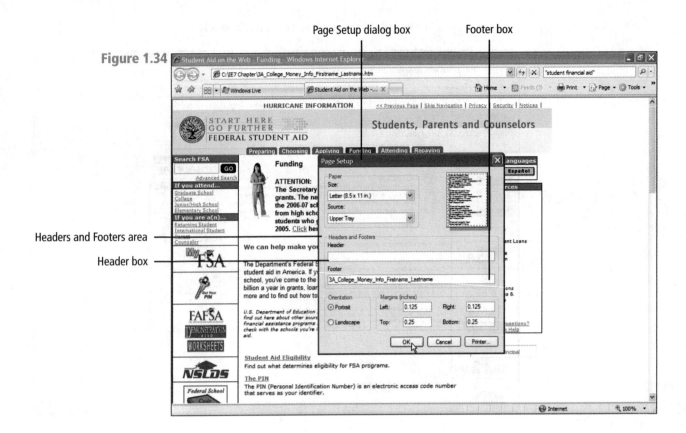

Headers and Footers area

Header box

▣ In the **Page Setup** dialog box, click **OK**. On the toolbar, click the **Print button down arrow**, click **Print**, and then at the bottom of the displayed Print dialog box, click the **Print** button.

The pages of the saved Web page print. It is likely that two or more pages will print. Each page will have the footer you created at the bottom.

▣ On the toolbar, click the **Home** button to display your home page.

Activity 1.14 Printing Web Graphics

When you print a Web page, you print all of the elements that make up that Web page, both the graphics and text. It is possible to print only the graphics that are part of the Web page. In this activity you will create a document with a graphic that you have saved from a Web page and print the document.

▣ From the **Start** menu, click **All Programs**, point to **Microsoft Office**, and then click **Microsoft Office Word 2007**.

Microsoft Office Word, a word processing program, will open a new document. You will add text and graphics to this new document.

▣ In the new **Word** document, type **1A_Career_Info_Firstname_ Lastname** and then press [Enter]. On the **Insert** tab, in the **Illustrations group**, point to **Picture** (but do not click). Compare your screen with Figure 1.35.

Figure 1.35

Insert tab   Picture button

Illustrations group

Text that has been added

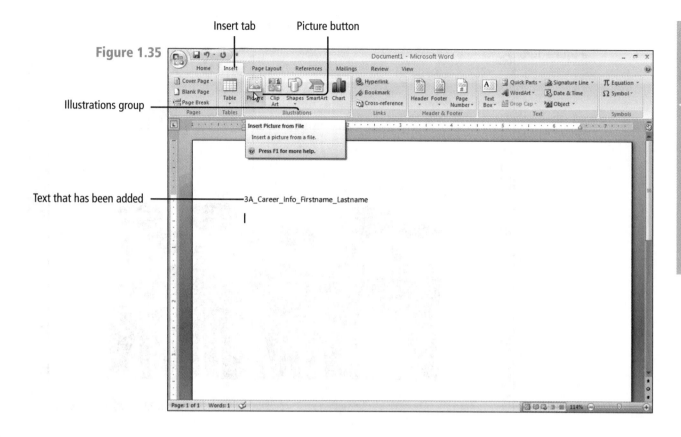

In the **Illustrations** group, click the **Picture** button to display the **Insert Picture** dialog box. Use the **Look in** box to locate the file **1A_Career_Info_Firstname_Lastname** in your **IE7 Chapter** folder. This graphic was downloaded in Activity 1.12.

In the **Insert Picture** dialog box, click the file name, and then click **Insert**.

The Web graphic displays underneath your text in the new document. Compare your screen with Figure 1.36.

Web graphic that has been inserted

Figure 1.36

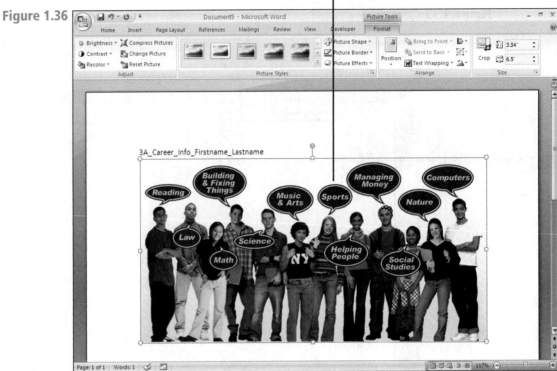

From the **Office** button [icon], click **Save As** and then navigate to your **IE7 Chapter** folder so that its name displays in the **Save in** box. At the bottom of the dialog box, click in the **File name** box to select the existing text, and then replace it by typing **1A_Career_Info_ Firstname_Lastname** Be sure to use your own first name and last name and insert underscores between words instead of spaces. Leave the **Save as type** box as the default type, and then in the lower right corner, click the **Save** button.

More Knowledge
Be Aware of Copyright Issues

Nearly everything you find on the Web is protected by copyright law, which protects authors of original works, including text, art, photographs, and music. If you want to use text or graphics that you find online, you will need to get permission. One of the exceptions to this law is the use of small amounts of information for educational purposes, which falls under Fair Use guidelines.

Copyright laws in the United States are open to different interpretations, and copyright laws can be very different in other countries. As a general rule, if you want to use someone else's material, always get permission first.

6. From the **Office** button 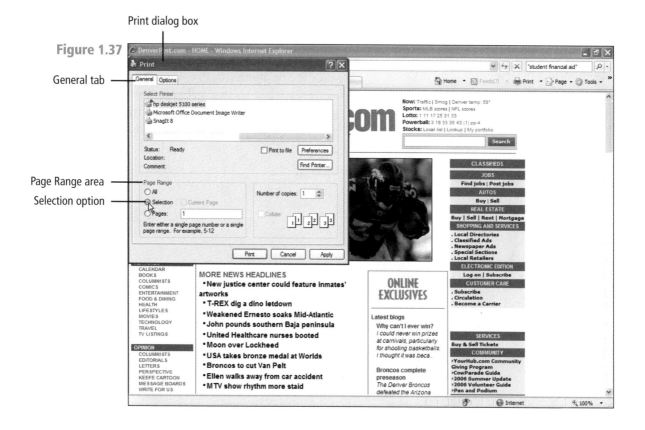, click **Print**, and then at the bottom of the displayed **Print** dialog box, click the **OK** button.

The document containing the saved Web graphic prints.

7. **Close** Word to return to the **Internet Explorer** window.

Activity 1.15 Printing Selected Text from Web Pages

1. In the **Address Bar** box, type **www.denverpost.com** and press Enter.

The Denver Post Web site displays current information and news items.

2. On the Web page, drag your mouse over the first paragraph to select it.

The paragraph will display as light text on a dark background.

3. On the toolbar, click the **Print** button down arrow, and then click **Print** to display the **Print** dialog box.

4. On the **General tab** of the **Print** dialog box, under **Page Range,** click the **Selection** option. Compare your screen with Figure 1.37. Click **Print**.

Internet Explorer prints only the selected text and not the entire Web page.

Print dialog box

Figure 1.37

General tab

Page Range area

Selection option

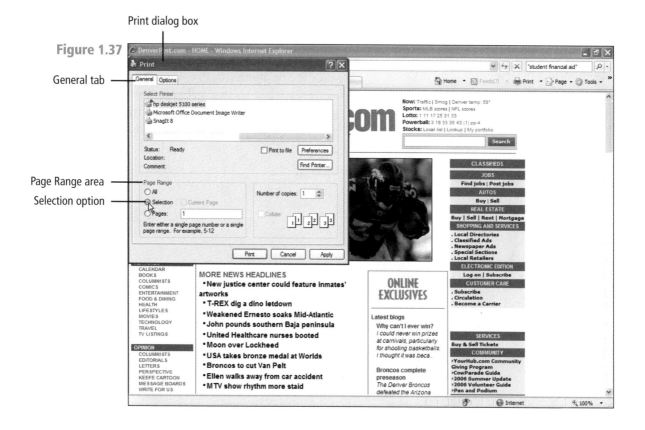

5 On the Internet Explorer title bar, click the program's **Close** button ☒.

6 Respond appropriately to messages, if prompted.

End **You have completed Project 1A** ————————————————

Content-Based Assessments

Summary

In this project, you explored basic features for starting Internet Explorer, navigating among Web pages, and working with Favorites. You learned how to search for Web sites containing information about topics you specify and how to download and save Web pages and graphics. You learned how to print a Web page, a graphic saved from a Web page, and selected text on a Web page.

Key Terms

Content-Based Assessments

Matching

Match each term in the second column with its correct definition in the first column by writing the letter of the term on the blank line in front of the correct definition.

_____ **1.** A software program that allows you to view the contents of the World Wide Web.

_____ **2.** A document on the World Wide Web that displays as a screen with associated links, frames, pictures, and other features of interest.

_____ **3.** A complete and unique Web site address.

_____ **4.** A company that provides access to the Internet.

_____ **5.** A place on the Internet that connects you to other sites.

_____ **6.** The Web page that opens each time you start Internet Explorer.

_____ **7.** Programs that search for keywords in files and documents or other Web sites found on the Internet.

_____ **8.** Distracting windows that display on your screen without you actually requesting them.

_____ **9.** A list that contains Web addresses for sites you plan to visit frequently.

_____ **10.** Separate areas of Web page content placed closely together with or without any visible demarcation lines so that all areas display as one page.

_____ **11.** A group of related pages on the Internet.

_____ **12.** Saving a copy of a Web page on your system or storage device.

_____ **13.** Text, buttons, pictures, or other objects displayed on Web pages that, when clicked, access other Web pages or display other sections of the active page.

A Downloading

B Favorites

C Frames

D Home page

E Hyperlinks

F Internet Service Provider (ISP)

G Pop-ups

H Portal

I Search engines

J Uniform Resource Locator (URL)

K Web browser

L Web page

M Web site

Content-Based Assessments

Fill in the Blank

Write the correct answer in the space provided.

1. Three characters that separate the protocol from the rest of the Web address are _____.

2. WWW stands for _____ _____ _____.

3. Government Web sites normally end with _____.

4. The Internet Explorer feature that tracks sites you visit over a period of time is the _____ feature.

5. The mouse pointer appears as a _____ _____ when you point to a hyperlink on a Web page.

6. To display the previous Web page, on the Standard Buttons toolbar, click _____.

7. The _____ is used to add a second Web site for viewing without closing the first Web site.

8. The portion of a Web address that follows the *www* and the name of the organization is called the _____.

9. Microsoft Internet Explorer is a software program called a(n) _____ that allows you to view the contents of the World Wide Web.

10. A _____ is a set of rules for transferring data over the Internet.

Content-Based Assessments

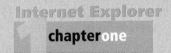

Skills Review

Project 1B—Playing Music from a Favorite Link

In this project, you will apply the skills you practiced from the Objectives in Project 1A.

Objectives: 1. *Start Internet Explorer 7.0 and Identify Screen Elements;* **2.** *Navigate the Internet;* **3.** *Create and Manage Favorites.*

In the following Skills Review project, you will open a Web site, save it in Favorites, and locate and listen to a radio station that is near Lake Michigan City College. You can use the radio tuner to locate radio stations in your area and, if you have a sound card, you can listen to the radio as you work. Your screen will look similar with Figure 1.38.

Figure 1.38

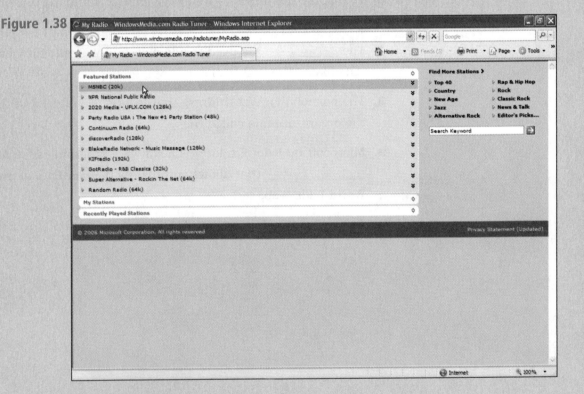

(Project 1B–Playing Music from a Favorite Link continues on the next page)

Content-Based Assessments

Skills Review

(Project 1B–Playing Music from a Favorite Link continued)

1. On the Windows taskbar, click the **Start** button, and then locate **Internet Explorer** on your system. On your system, click **Internet Explorer**. In the **Address bar**, type **http://windowsmedia.com/radiotuner** Press [Enter].

2. On the toolbar, click the **Add to Favorites** button, and then click **Add to Favorites** to display the **Add a Favorite** dialog box.

3. In the **Add a Favorite** dialog box, change the name to **Radio Station Guide** and then click the **Add** button.

Each radio station in the Featured Stations can be expanded to display additional links. You can use the additional links to add a radio station in the My Stations list for easier access, or to play the station. You can locate more stations by using the **Find More Stations** link, and you can locate stations that you listened to recently in the *Recently Played Stations* list.

4. In the **Featured Stations** list, click **MSNBC** to expand the listing.

5. Under the **MSNBC** listing, click the **Play** link to play the station.

The Windows Media Player opens and the station plays. This may take a few seconds as the streaming process occurs. Depending on the active settings on your system, Internet Explorer may present a message box asking if you want to play the station in Internet Explorer. Notice the buttons to stop the music and to close the Media window when you are done listening.

6. Click **Yes** to play the station from Internet Explorer, if prompted. If you have a sound card, live radio from MSNBC plays.

7. In the **Windows Media Player** window, click the **Stop** button to stop the live broadcast, and then click the Media pane's **Close** button to close the pane.

8. Click the **Close** button to close Internet Explorer.

End **You have completed Project 1B** ⎯⎯⎯⎯⎯⎯⎯⎯⎯⎯⎯⎯⎯⎯⎯⎯⎯⎯

Content-Based Assessments

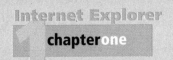
Project 1C—Searching for Multimedia

In this project, you will apply the skills you practiced from the Objectives in Project 1A.

Objectives: 1. *Start Internet Explorer 7.0 and Identify Screen Elements;* **4.** *Search the Internet;* **5.** *Save and Print Web Pages.*

In the following Skills Review, you will search for free downloads of multimedia for your music appreciation class at Lake Michigan City College.

The Internet provides opportunities to locate and download several types of multimedia, such as animated graphics and sound or video files. However, the ease with which it is possible to copy these files does not always make it legally acceptable. The Fair Use Guidelines for Educational Multimedia allow for the use of copyrighted materials for educational purposes under certain circumstances. These circumstances address the purpose of use and the quantity of materials to be used. In addition, consideration must be given to whether the work has been made public, and there must be no effect on any potential market. Follow these instructions to perform a search for free multimedia.

For Project 1C, you will need the following file:

New blank file

You will save your document as
1C_Multimedia_Firstname_Lastname

(Project 1C–Searching for Multimedia continues on the next page)

Content-Based Assessments

(Project 1C–Searching for Multimedia continued)

1. On the Windows taskbar, click the **Start** button, and then locate Internet Explorer on your system. On your system, click **Internet Explorer**.

2. On the toolbar, in the **Search** box, type **"Free Sound Files"** and then press Enter.

   Several Web sites that offer free and royalty-free sound files display. The file types for sound files include WAV files, MIDI files, and MP3 files.

3. Click the first link in the list of Web Results to display a Web site providing free sound files. Scroll down the Web page until you locate links on that Web page that lead to any file type.

4. On the link leading to a sound file, move your mouse until it displays as a **Link Select pointer** 🖑 and right-click to reveal a context-sensitive menu.

5. From the context-sensitive menu, click **Save Target As** to display the **Save As**

dialog box. In the **File name** box, type **1C_Multimedia_Firstname_Lastname** In the **Save in** box, navigate to the **IE7 Chapter** folder that you created earlier in this chapter.

6. In the **Save As** dialog box, click **Save**.

7. In the **Download complete** dialog box, click the **Close** button.

   You will return to the Web page where you located the sound file.

8. In the **Address** bar, type the drive (i.e., **c:**) and the location **IE7 Chapter** where you saved the file, and the most recent files in that location will display. Scroll down as necessary, and click the file name that you saved in Step 5.

9. On the toolbar, click **Print** to open the **Print** dialog box. Click the **Print** button to print the saved Web page. **Close** Internet Explorer.

End **You have completed Project 1C**

Content-Based Assessments

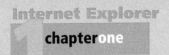
Mastering Internet Explorer

Project 1D—Searching for Picture Space

In this project, you will apply the skills you practiced from the Objectives in Project 1A.

Objectives: 1. *Start Internet Explorer 7.0 and Identify Screen Elements;* **4.** *Search the Internet;* **5.** *Save and Print Web Pages.*

> **For Project 1D, you will need the following file:**

New blank file

You will save your document as
1D_Picture Space_Firstname_Lastname

In this project, you will search for free photographic services for the Alumni Club at Lake Michigan City College. The festivities on Homecoming Weekend were a great success and brought in alumni from around the state. Many sites on the Internet offer free space for storing and sharing pictures. From these sites, friends and family can view pictures and order copies of those pictures they want to keep. You can locate these services by searching the Internet. Follow these steps to locate and explore sites to determine which one best meets your needs.

(Project 1D–Searching for Picture Space continues on the next page)

Content-Based Assessments

Mastering Internet Explorer

(Project 1D–Searching for Picture Space continued)

1. Open **Internet Explorer**.

2. On the toolbar, in the **Search** box, type **"free online photo albums"** and then press [Enter]. Several Web sites that offer free photographic services, such as storage and online photo albums, display.

3. Click the first link in the list of **Web Results** to display a Web site providing a free online photo album that is not a sponsored site. Scroll down the Web page until you locate information about how that online photo album works.

4. On the toolbar, click the **Page** button, and then click **Save As** to display the **Save Webpage** dialog box. In the **File name** box, type **1D_Photo_Site_1_Firstname_Lastname** Change the **Save as type** to **Webpage, complete**, and then in the **Save in** box, navigate to the **IE7 Chapter** folder that you created earlier in the chapter.

5. In the **Save Webpage** dialog box, click **Save**. The dialog box will close and the file will be saved. Click the **Back** button to return to the search results.

6. Click another link in the list of Web Results to display another Web site providing a free online photo album. Scroll down that Web page until you locate information about how that online photo album works.

7. On the toolbar, click the **Page** button, and then click **Save As** to display the **Save Webpage** dialog box. In the **File name** box, type **1D_Photo_Site_2_Firstname_Lastname** Change the **Save as type** to **Webpage, complete**, and then in the **Save in** box, navigate to the **IE7 Chapter** folder that you created earlier in the chapter.

8. In the **Save Webpage** dialog box, click **Save**. The dialog box will close and the file will be saved.

9. Use the address bar to open each of the two saved files and then on the toolbar, click the **Print** button to print each of the saved files.

10. **Close** all files and **Close** Internet Explorer.

End You have completed Project 1D

Content-Based Assessments

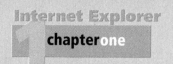

Project 1E — Locating Free Items

In this project, you will apply the skills you practiced from the Objectives in Project 1A.

Objectives: 1. *Start Internet Explorer 7.0 and Identify Screen Elements;* **3.** *Create and Manage Favorites;* **4.** *Search the Internet.*

In the following project, you will search for free coupons, offers, and programs available on the Internet as marketing giveaway items for your club at Lake Michigan City College. As you become more familiar with the Internet, you will run across a large amount of free items such as software programs, computer equipment, computer services, and so forth— available from Web sites. Unfortunately, not all of these offers are legitimate. Search the Internet for free items and review some of the offers. As you explore and evaluate the sites, remember that you should download programs and information only from sites you know and trust. See if you can determine which sites make legitimate offers and which do not. Several criteria may help you with this determination. The following set of questions will be helpful as you perform an evaluation of a Web site:

- Is the site attractive and professional looking?

- When was the last time that the Web site was updated? Are there broken links or misspelled words?

- Who owns or sponsors the site? Do they seem qualified to make this type of offer?

- Are you required to provide personal data such as name, location, age, or credit or financial information in order to receive "free" items?

(Project 1E–Locating Free Items continues on the next page)

Content-Based Assessments

Mastering Internet Explorer

(Project 1E–Locating Free Items continued)

1. Open **Internet Explorer**.

2. On the toolbar, in the **Search** box, type "free stuff" and then press Enter.

3. Click on the first link in the list of **Web Results** to display a Web site providing free stuff that is not a sponsored site. Scroll down the Web page until you locate the answers to the set of questions in the previous list to help you determine the legitimacy of the free offers.

4. On the toolbar, click the **Add to Favorites** button, and then click **Add to Favorites** to open the **Add a Favorite** dialog box.

5. In the **Add a Favorite** dialog box, click the **New Folder** button. In the **Folder name** box, type **Free Stuff** Click **Create**, and then click **Add** to add the Web site to the folder. A new folder named Free Stuff displays in the list of Favorites and the current Web site has been added to it.

6. On the toolbar, click **Back** to return to the **Web Results**. Scroll down the list to choose another Web site offering free stuff. Click the link to that Web site and answer the same set of questions to determine the legitimacy of the free offers.

7. On the toolbar, click the **Add to Favorites** button, and then click **Add to Favorites** to open the **Add a Favorite** dialog box. Be sure the **Free Stuff** folder is displayed in the **Create in** box, and then click the **Add** button.

8. On the toolbar, click the **Favorites Center** button, scroll down, and then click on the **Free Stuff** folder to display the two Web sites that you added to the folder.

9. Click anywhere outside the **Favorites** list to close it, and then **Close** Internet Explorer.

End You have completed Project 1E

Content-Based Assessments

Project 1F— Protecting Your Privacy

In this project, you will apply the skills you practiced from the Objectives in Project 1A.

Objectives: 1. *Start Internet Explorer 7.0 and Identify Screen Elements;* **4.** *Search the Internet;* **5.** *Save and Print Web Pages.*

For Project 1F, you will need the following file:

New blank file

You will save your document as
1F_Privacy_Firstname_Lastname

In this project, you will search the Internet for information about yourself or other members of your family as part of your sociology project at Lake Michigan City College. The World Wide Web stores information about individuals in addition to companies. Many businesses store data about their clients and customers in databases on the Web so that they can place orders online. Families often store family trees on Web sites so that others can track their family history. Search the Internet for information about yourself to see what information is stored about you and others with your name. You may prefer to search for information about your family name to see if family tree data is available. The World Wide Web provides a means to easily gather personal information about you and your family. One of the best ways to protect your family and yourself is to look at the privacy policies of Web sites that you visit. Locate and review the privacy policy at any Web site you found that contains information about you or your family. Answer these questions:

- How does the Web site collect information about you?

- How is the information used?

- Are there options for you to prevent the collection and sharing of your personal data?

(Project 1F–Protecting Your Privacy continues on the next page)

Content-Based Assessments

(Project 1F–Protecting Your Privacy continued)

1. Open **Internet Explorer**.

2. In the **Address Bar** box, type **www.anywho. com** and then press [Enter]. The AnyWho Online Directory displays.

3. In the **Find a Person** section, type your last name and your first name or another family member's name. Then choose your state from the drop down list. Click the **Search** button. A number of results will be returned.

4. Scroll down to the bottom of the results page. Click the **Privacy Policy** link. Read the privacy policy to determine the answers to the set of questions listed earlier.

5. On the toolbar, click the **Page** button, and then click **Save As** to display the **Save Webpage** dialog box. In the **File name** box, type **1F_Privacy_1_Firstname_Lastname** If necessary, change the **Save as type** to **Web Archive, single file**, and then in the **Save in** box, navigate to the **IE7 Chapter** folder that you created earlier in the chapter. If you are unable to save this Web site, proceed to Step 6.

6. In the **Address Bar** box, type **www. whitepages.com** and then press [Enter] to

display the **WhitePages.com** home page.

7. In the **People Search** section, type your first name, last name, and your state in the appropriate boxes. Click the **Search** button. A number of results are displayed.

8. Scroll down to the bottom of the results page. Click the **Privacy Policy** link. Read the privacy policy to determine the answers to the questions listed at the beginning of this project.

9. On the toolbar, click the **Page** button, and then click **Save As** to display the **Save Webpage** dialog box. In the **File name** box, type **1F_Privacy_2_Firstname_Lastname** If necessary, change the **Save as type** to **Web Archive, single file**, and in the **Save in** box, navigate to the **IE7 Chapter** folder that you created earlier in the chapter.

10. Use the address bar to open each of the two saved files and then on the toolbar, use the **Print** button to print each of the saved files.

11. **Close** all files, and then **Close** Internet Explorer.

End You have completed Project 1F

Outcomes-Based Assessments

Rubric

The following Outcomes-Based Assessments are *open-ended assessments*. That is, there is no specific correct result; your result will depend on your approach to the information provided. Make *Professional Quality* your goal. Use the following scoring rubric to guide you in *how* to approach the problem and then to evaluate *how well* your approach solves the problem.

The *criteria*—Software Mastery, Content, Format and Layout, and Process—represent the knowledge and skills you have gained that you can apply to solving the problem. The *levels of performance*—Professional Quality, Approaching Professional Quality, or Needs Quality Improvements—help you and your instructor evaluate your result.

	Your completed project is of Professional Quality if you:	Your completed project is Approaching Professional Quality if you:	Your completed project Needs Quality Improvements if you:
1-Software Mastery	Choose and apply the most appropriate skills, tools, and features and identify efficient methods to solve the problem.	Choose and apply some appropriate skills, tools, and features, but not in the most efficient manner.	Choose inappropriate skills, tools, or features, or are inefficient in solving the problem.
2-Content	Construct a solution that is clear and well organized, contains content that is accurate, appropriate to the audience and purpose, and is complete. Provide a solution that contains no errors of spelling, grammar, or style.	Construct a solution in which some components are unclear, poorly organized, inconsistent, or incomplete. Misjudge the needs of the audience. Have some errors in spelling, grammar, or style, but the errors do not detract from comprehension.	Construct a solution that is unclear, incomplete, or poorly organized, containing some inaccurate or inappropriate content; and contains many errors of spelling, grammar, or style. Do not solve the problem.
3-Format and Layout	Format and arrange all elements to communicate information and ideas, clarify function, illustrate relationships, and indicate relative importance.	Apply appropriate format and layout features to some elements, but not others. Overuse features, causing minor distraction.	Apply format and layout that does not communicate information or ideas clearly. Do not use format and layout features to clarify function, illustrate relationships, or indicate relative importance. Use available features excessively, causing distraction.
4-Process	Use an organized approach that integrates planning, development, self-assessment, revision, and reflection.	Demonstrate an organized approach in some areas, but not others; or, use an insufficient process of organization throughout.	Do not use an organized approach to solve the problem.

Problem Solving

Project 1G — Exploring Copyright Laws

In this project, you will construct a solution by applying any combination of the Objectives found in Project 1A.

For Project 1G, you will need the following file:

New blank file

**You will save your document as
1G_Copyright Laws_Firstname_Lastname**

Use the skills you practiced in this chapter to locate information on copyright laws and the appropriate use of copyrighted information for educational purposes. The major focus of legislation in this area includes findings on the Digital Millennium Act, the TEACH Act, and Fair Use.

Conduct a search to locate the Web site of the government organization that oversees copyright law or a Web site of an educational institution that pertains to this topic area. Explore that Web site to locate information on each of the three findings named earlier. Save the Digital Distance Education Web page as **1G_Digital_Firstname_Lastname** Save the TEACH Act Web page as **1G_Teach_2_Firstname_Lastname** Save the Fair Use Web page as **1G_Fair_Use_Firstname_Lastname** Print each Web page and submit the documents as directed.

End **You have completed Project 1G** ──────────

Glossary

Animated banner A series of rotating or changing text and images embedded within the Web page.

Downloading The action of requesting and copying a file or program from a remote server, such as a Web server, and saving it on your local computer or storage device.

Favorites Center An area in Internet Explorer that lets you manage your favorites list, the history list, and the feeds list.

Frames Separate areas of content placed closely together so they will display as one unified Web page with or without any visible demarcation lines between them.

History A feature of Internet Explorer that tracks recently visited Web pages and sites.

Home page The Web page that displays every time you start Internet Explorer.

Hyperlinks Text, buttons, pictures, or other objects displayed on Web pages that, when clicked, access other Web pages or display other sections of the active page.

Internet Explorer 7.0 A software program that allows you to view the contents of the World Wide Web.

Internet Service Provider (ISP) A company that provides an Internet connection through a regular telephone line, a special high-speed telephone line, or a cable.

Link Select pointer The mouse pointer displaying as a pointing hand as you point to an item that links to another Web page.

Pop-up blocker A command on the Tools menu that stops or allows pop-ups to display as you browse the Internet.

Pop-ups Small windows that display on your screen without you actually requesting them as your browse the Internet.

Portals Home pages that act as launching sites to other Web pages, for example containing links to access frequently visited sites, up-to-the-minute news, weather reports, and maps and directories.

Protocol A set of rules for transferring data over the Internet.

ScreenTip A small box that displays useful information when you perform various mouse actions such as pointing to screen elements or dragging.

Search Engines Software programs that search for keywords in files and documents or other Web sites found on the Internet.

Sponsored links Web sites that pay to be prominently displayed as results at a search engine site.

Tabs A feature of Internet Explorer 7.0 that allows multiple Web pages to be displayed at the same time without opening multiple browsers.

Uniform Resource Locator (URL) The unique address used to locate a Web page or Web site.

Web browser Software that enables you to use the Web and navigate from page to page and site to site.

Web page A document on the World Wide Web that displays as a screen with associated links, frames, pictures, and other features of interest.

Web site A group of related Web pages published to a specific location on the World Wide Web.

Index

:// , 11

A

Add to Favorites button, 6–7, 24–25, 26, 47, 53
Address bar, 7, 11–12
animated banners, 13

B

Back button, 8, 53

C

categories of information, 7
Close button, 7
Close tab button, 16
copyright issues
  information, finding on Internet, 57
  Web graphics, 40

D

dates, displaying in History, 21–22
default Internet search provider, creating, 29
Delete button, Favorites, 27
domain name, 11
downloading
  software, 35
  Web pages, 31–32
drives, navigating to, 32, 34

F

Favorites
  address, adding, 6–7, 24–25
  deleting address from, 26–28
  displaying site, 25–26
  playing music, 46–47
Favorites Center, 13, 21, 25–26
Forward button, 8
frames, Web page, 34

H

Header/Footer tab, Internet Explorer, 37
History feature, 21
Home button, 9
home page, 5, 8
http, 11

I

Internet connection, 5
Internet Explorer 7.0
  described, 2, 4
  Favorites
    address, adding, 6–7, 24–25
    deleting address from, 26–28
    displaying site, 25–26
    playing music, 46–47
  home page, 5
  Internet connection, 5
  navigating Internet
    History feature, 21–23
    hyperlinks, displaying Web pages with, 16–21
    second Web site, opening, 15–16
    Toolbar commands, 8–9
    Web sites, accessing from Address Bar, 9–14
  portals, 8
  saving Web pages, 31–35
    downloading graphics, 35–36
    downloading new programs, 35
    printing, 36–38
    printing graphics, 38–41
    printing selected text, 41–42
  screen elements, 7
  searching Internet
    beginning, 29–30
    for free coupons, offers, and programs, 52–53
    for free photographic services, 50–51
    for multimedia, 48–49
    for yourself and members of your family, 54–55
    returning to search results, 31
    search engines, 28–29
    sponsored links, 30
  starting, 4–5
  Web page, 5
  Web site, 5
Internet Service Provider (ISP), 5

L

Link Select pointer, 16, 49
links, 7

M

Minimize button, 7
mouse pointer, 7
My Computer, printing Web pages, 36–37